Photoshop CS
Advanced

Student Manual

ACE Edition

Photoshop CS3: Advanced

President & Chief Executive Officer:	Michael Springer
Vice President, Product Development:	Adam A. Wilcox
Vice President, Operations:	Josh Pincus
Director of Publishing Systems Development:	Dan Quackenbush
Writer:	Chris Hale
Developmental Editor:	Jim O'Shea
Series Designer:	Adam A. Wilcox

Trademarks

ILT Series is a trademark of Axzo Press.

Some of the product names and company names used in this book have been used for identification purposes only and may be trademarks or registered trademarks of their respective manufacturers and sellers.

Disclaimers

We reserve the right to revise this publication and make changes from time to time in its content without notice.

The Adobe Approved Certification Courseware logo is either a registered trademark or trademark of Adobe Systems Incorporated in the United States and/or other countries. The Adobe Approved Certification Courseware logo is a proprietary trademark of Adobe. All rights reserved.

The ILT Series is independent from ProCert Labs, LLC and Adobe Systems Incorporated, and are not affiliated with ProCert Labs and Adobe in any manner. This publication may assist students to prepare for an Adobe Certified Expert exam, however, neither ProCert Labs nor Adobe warrant that use of this material will ensure success in connection with any exam.

Student Manual
ISBN-10: 1-4260-9475-2
ISBN-13: 978-1-4260-9475-0

Student Manual with data CD
ISBN-10: 1-4260-9477-9
ISBN-13: 978-1-4260-9477-4

Printed in the United States of America

1 2 3 4 5 6 7 8 9 10 GL 10 09 08

Contents

Course summary   S-1

Quick reference   Q-1

Glossary   G-1

Index   I-1

Introduction

After reading this introduction, you will know how to:

A Use ILT Series manuals in general.

B Use prerequisites, a target student description, course objectives, and a skills inventory to properly set your expectations for the course.

C Re-key this course after class.

Topic A: About the manual

ILT Series philosophy

ILT Series manuals facilitate your learning by providing structured interaction with the software itself. While we provide text to explain difficult concepts, the hands-on activities are the focus of our courses. By paying close attention as your instructor leads you through these activities, you will learn the skills and concepts effectively.

We believe strongly in the instructor-led class. During class, focus on your instructor. Our manuals are designed and written to facilitate your interaction with your instructor, and not to call attention to manuals themselves.

We believe in the basic approach of setting expectations, delivering instruction, and providing summary and review afterwards. For this reason, lessons begin with objectives and end with summaries. We also provide overall course objectives and a course summary to provide both an introduction to and closure on the entire course.

Manual components

The manuals contain these major components:

- Table of contents
- Introduction
- Units
- Appendix
- Course summary
- Quick reference
- Glossary
- Index

Each element is described below.

Table of contents

The table of contents acts as a learning roadmap.

Introduction

The introduction contains information about our training philosophy and our manual components, features, and conventions. It contains target student, prerequisite, objective, and setup information for the specific course.

Units

Units are the largest structural component of the course content. A unit begins with a title page that lists objectives for each major subdivision, or topic, within the unit. Within each topic, conceptual and explanatory information alternates with hands-on activities. Units conclude with a summary comprising one paragraph for each topic, and an independent practice activity that gives you an opportunity to practice the skills you've learned.

The conceptual information takes the form of text paragraphs, exhibits, lists, and tables. The activities are structured in two columns, one telling you what to do, the other providing explanations, descriptions, and graphics.

Appendices

The appendix for this course lists the Adobe Certified Expert (ACE) exam objectives for Photoshop CS3, along with references to corresponding coverage in ILT Series courseware.

Course summary

This section provides a text summary of the entire course. It is useful for providing closure at the end of the course. The course summary also indicates the next course in this series, if there is one, and lists additional resources you might find useful as you continue to learn about the software.

Quick reference

The quick reference is an at-a-glance job aid summarizing some of the more common features of the software.

Glossary

The glossary provides definitions for all of the key terms used in this course.

Index

The index at the end of this manual makes it easy for you to find information about a particular software component, feature, or concept.

Manual conventions

We've tried to keep the number of elements and the types of formatting to a minimum in the manuals. This aids in clarity and makes the manuals more classically elegant looking. But there are some conventions and icons you should know about.

Item	Description
Italic text	In conceptual text, indicates a new term or feature.
Bold text	In unit summaries, indicates a key term or concept. In an independent practice activity, indicates an explicit item that you select, choose, or type.
`Code font`	Indicates code or syntax.
`Longer strings of ▶ code will look ▶ like this.`	In the hands-on activities, any code that's too long to fit on a single line is divided into segments by one or more continuation characters (▶). This code should be entered as a continuous string of text.
Select **bold item**	In the left column of hands-on activities, bold sans-serif text indicates an explicit item that you select, choose, or type.
Keycaps like ⏎ ENTER	Indicate a key on the keyboard you must press.

Hands-on activities

The hands-on activities are the most important parts of our manuals. They are divided into two primary columns. The "Here's how" column gives short instructions to you about what to do. The "Here's why" column provides explanations, graphics, and clarifications. Here's a sample:

Do it!

A-1: Creating a commission formula

Here's how	Here's why
1 Open Sales	This is an oversimplified sales compensation worksheet. It shows sales totals, commissions, and incentives for five sales reps.
2 Observe the contents of cell F4	F4 ▼ ═ =E4*C_Rate The commission rate formulas use the name "C_Rate" instead of a value for the commission rate.

For these activities, we have provided a collection of data files designed to help you learn each skill in a real-world business context. As you work through the activities, you will modify and update these files. Of course, you might make a mistake and therefore want to re-key the activity starting from scratch. To make it easy to start over, you will rename each data file at the end of the first activity in which the file is modified. Our convention for renaming files is to add the word "My" to the beginning of the file name. In the above activity, for example, a file called "Sales" is being used for the first time. At the end of this activity, you would save the file as "My sales," thus leaving the "Sales" file unchanged. If you make a mistake, you can start over using the original "Sales" file.

In some activities, however, it might not be practical to rename the data file. If you want to retry one of these activities, ask your instructor for a fresh copy of the original data file.

Topic B: Setting your expectations

Properly setting your expectations is essential to your success. This topic will help you do that by providing:

- Prerequisites for this course
- A description of the target student
- A list of the objectives for the course
- A skills assessment for the course

Course prerequisites

Before taking this course, you should be familiar with personal computers and the use of a keyboard and a mouse. Furthermore, this course assumes that you've completed the following courses or have equivalent experience:

- *Windows XP: Basic*
- *Photoshop CS3: Basic, ACE Edition*

Target student

The target student for this course is familiar with the basics of using Adobe Photoshop to create and modify digital images. You want to learn additional techniques for creating image effects.

Adobe ACE certification

This course is designed to help you pass the Adobe Certified Expert (ACE) exam for Photoshop CS3. For complete certification training, you should complete this course and all of the following:

- *Photoshop CS3: Basic, ACE Edition*
- *Photoshop CS3: Color Printing, ACE Edition*
- *Photoshop CS3: Web Design, ACE Edition*

Course objectives

These overall course objectives will give you an idea about what to expect from the course. It is also possible that they will help you see that this course is not the right one for you. If you think you either lack the prerequisite knowledge or already know most of the subject matter to be covered, you should let your instructor know that you think you are misplaced in the class.

Note: In addition to the general objectives listed below, specific ACE exam objectives are listed at the beginning of each topic. For a complete mapping of ACE objectives to ILT Series content, see Appendix A.

After completing this course, you will know how to:

- Add colors to the Swatches palette; apply colors to selections and as fill layers; apply patterns and gradients; use the Preset Manager to save presets; and apply colors and gradients by using overlay layer styles.

- Paint in Quick Mask mode and in an alpha channel to specify a selection; create layer masks to hide layer content; create grayscale masks to partially mask part of an image; and use a clipping mask to conform one layer to the shape of another.

- Use the path tools and commands to create and edit vector paths; use paths to create vector masks and clipping paths; convert type to paths and wrap type along a path; and use paths to create vector-based artwork.

- Use painting tools, filters, and blending modes to simulate different media; warp text and layers; group layers and create Smart Objects; apply Smart Filters and mask Smart Filter effects; create layer comps; and import, transform, and edit textures on 3D layers.

- Prepare images for use in video productions; open QuickTime video content in video layers; and edit video-frame content.

- Use the Actions palette to record, play, and edit actions; display actions as buttons and organize actions into action sets; use actions to batch-process images; and customize keyboard shortcuts and menus.

Skills inventory

Use the following form to gauge your skill level entering the class. For each skill listed, rate your familiarity from 1 to 5, with five being the most familiar. *This is not a test.* Rather, it is intended to provide you with an idea of where you're starting from at the beginning of class. If you're wholly unfamiliar with all the skills, you might not be ready for the class. If you think you already understand all of the skills, you might need to move on to the next course in the series. In either case, you should let your instructor know as soon as possible.

Skill	1	2	3	4	5
Creating color swatches and applying colors					
Creating fill layers					
Applying gradients and patterns					
Using the Preset Manager to save presets					
Filling areas with color overlays					
Creating and modifying selections by using Quick Mask mode and alpha channels					
Creating and editing layer masks					
Creating clipping masks					
Creating and modifying vector paths					
Creating vector masks and clipping paths					
Converting type to paths and wrapping it on paths					
Stroking a path with a brush shape					
Creating vector shape layers					
Drawing with the Art History Brush tool					
Blending a texture with Overlay mode					
Warping text layers and image content					
Grouping layers					
Creating and transforming Smart Objects					
Applying filters as Smart Filters					
Creating layer comps					
Importing, transforming, and editing textures on 3D layers					

Skill	1	2	3	4	5
Editing video frames in video layers					
Preparing images so they won't appear distorted in video productions					
Creating, playing, modifying, organizing, and batch-processing actions					
Customizing keyboard shortcuts and menu displays					

Topic C: Re-keying the course

If you have the proper hardware and software, you can re-key this course after class. This section explains what you'll need in order to do so, and how to do it.

Hardware requirements

Your personal computer should have:

- A keyboard and a mouse
- Intel Pentium 4, Intel Centrino, Intel Xeon, or Intel Core Duo (or compatible) processor
- 512 MB of RAM
- 3GB of available hard disk space
- A DVD-ROM drive
- An XGA or better monitor with 32-bit color support (1024x768 resolution)

Software requirements

You will also need the following software:

- Windows XP with Service Pack 2. (You can also use Windows Vista Home Premium, Business, Ultimate, or Enterprise, although the screen shots in this course were taken using Windows XP, so your screens might look somewhat different.)
- Adobe Photoshop CS3.
- Adobe Reader is required to complete Activity E-1 ("Creating layer comps") in the unit titled "Creative image effects." You can download Adobe Reader for free from www.adobe.com.

Network requirements

The following network components and connectivity are also required for rekeying this course:

- Internet access, for the following purposes:
  - Downloading the latest critical updates and service packs from www.windowsupdate.com
  - Downloading Adobe Reader from www.adobe.com
  - Downloading the Student Data files (if necessary)

Setup instructions to re-key the course

Before you re-key the course, you will need to perform the following steps.

1   Download the latest critical updates and service packs from www.windowsupdate.com.

2   From the Control Panel, open the Display Properties dialog box and apply the following settings:

- Theme — Windows XP
- Screen resolution — 1024 by 768 pixels
- Color quality — High (24 bit) or higher

If you choose not to apply these display settings, your screens might not match the screen shots in this manual.

3   If necessary, reset any Photoshop CS3 defaults that you have changed. If you do not wish to reset the defaults, you can still re-key the course, but some activities might not work exactly as documented.

   a   While holding Ctrl+Alt+Shift, start Photoshop. This will open a dialog box through which you can return Photoshop to its default configuration.

   b   Click Yes to delete the Adobe Photoshop Settings file.

   c   Choose Window, Workspace, Delete Workspace to open the Delete Workspace dialog box. From the Workspace list, select Action Editing. Click Delete and then click Yes.

   d   Choose Window, Workspace, Keyboard Shortcuts & Menus to open the Keyboard Shortcuts and Menus dialog box. Activate the Keyboard Shortcuts tab. From the Set list, select Action editing shortcuts. Click the Delete button and click Yes.

   e   In the Keyboard Shortcuts and Menus dialog box, activate the Menus tab. From the Set list, select Action editing menus. Click the Delete button and click Yes.

   f   Close Photoshop.

4   Configure Photoshop CS3 as follows:

   a   Start Adobe Photoshop CS3. At the Welcome screen, click Close.

   b   Choose Edit, Preferences, File Handling. Set Maximize PSD File Compatibility to Always. Click OK.

   c   Close Photoshop.

5   Create a folder named Student Data at the root of the hard drive. For a standard hard drive setup, this will be C:\Student Data.

6   Download the Student Data files for the course. (If you do not have an Internet connection, you can ask your instructor for a copy of the data files on a disk.)

   a   Connect to www.axzopress.com.

   b   Under Downloads, click Instructor-Led Training.

   c   Browse the subject categories to locate your course. Then click the course title to display a list of available downloads. (You can also access these downloads through our Catalog listings.)

   d   Click the link(s) for downloading the Student Data files, and follow the instructions that appear on your screen.

7   Copy the data files to the Student Data folder.

CertBlaster exam preparation for ACE certification

You can download CertBlaster exam preparation software for ACE certification from our Web site. To do so:

1 Go to www.axzopress.com.

2 Under Downloads, click CertBlaster.

3 Click the link for Photoshop CS3.

4 Save the .EXE file to a folder on your hard drive. (**Note:** If you skip this step, the CertBlaster software will not install correctly.)

5 Click Start and choose Run.

6 Click Browse and then navigate to the folder that contains the .EXE file.

7 Select the .EXE file and click Open.

8 Click OK and follow the on-screen instructions. When prompted for the password, enter **c_pscs3**.

Unit 1

Fills and overlays

Unit time: 70 minutes

Complete this unit, and you'll know how to:

A Specify colors and store them in the Swatches palette, and apply colors to image selections and as fill layers.

B Apply fill types such as patterns and gradients, and use the Preset Manager to save presets.

C Use overlay layer styles to apply colors and gradients to layer content.

Topic A: Filling image areas

This topic covers the following Adobe ACE exam objective for Photoshop CS3.

#	Objective
5.1	Given a scenario create a new document by selecting the appropriate document preset.

Applying color

Explanation

As you create and modify images and artwork, you can apply color to selected image areas. To specify a color, you can use the Color palette, the Color Picker dialog box, or the Eyedropper tool.

If you're using the same colors repeatedly, however, you should save them as swatches in the Swatches palette so you won't need to redefine or resample them each time you want to apply them. In addition, when you want to fill a layer with a solid color, a gradient, or a pattern, you should do so by creating a fill layer.

The Swatches palette

The Swatches palette displays a set of swatches as small color squares by default. You can display a different set of swatches by selecting one from the Swatches palette menu. For example, you can select Pantone colors, Web-safe colors, and more. In addition, you can customize the Swatches palette by adding your own colors. You can also change how the swatches are displayed in the palette. For example, you can select Small List from the Swatches palette menu to display the swatches with their names as a list, as shown in Exhibit 1-1.

To add a color to the Swatches palette:

1 Specify the foreground color by using the Color palette, the Eyedropper tool, or the Color Picker dialog box.

2 Add the color to the Swatches palette by using either of these techniques:

- Point to an empty area at the bottom of the Swatches palette, so the pointer appears as a paint bucket, and click. In the Color Swatch Name dialog box that appears, enter a name and click OK.

- Click the "Create new swatch of foreground color" button at the bottom of the Swatches palette. Double-click the new swatch to open the Color Swatch Name dialog box; then enter a name and click OK. (You can also press Alt as you click the "Create new swatch of foreground color" button to automatically open the Color Swatch Name dialog box.)

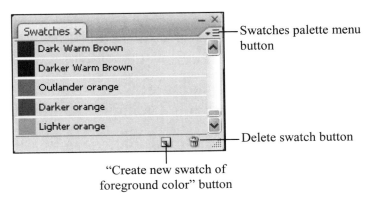

Swatches palette menu button

Delete swatch button

"Create new swatch of foreground color" button

Exhibit 1-1: The Swatches palette displayed in Small List view

If you want to remove a swatch from the Swatches palette, you can drag the swatch to the Delete swatch icon, or press Alt and click the swatch.

HSB color

You can use the Color palette to specify colors by using a variety of color models, such as RGB, CMYK, or grayscale. Some people prefer to define color by using the HSB (hue, saturation, brightness) color model, which many find to be more intuitive. The HSB color model's range is similar to RGB's, but HSB defines colors based on their hue, saturation, and brightness, as shown in Exhibit 1-2.

The hue value is measured in degrees, based on the concept of all available hues being displayed on a circle known as a *color wheel*. Each degree in the circle represents a different hue along a spectrum. The saturation and brightness values are measured in percentages.

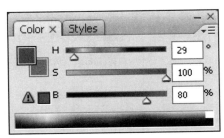

Exhibit 1-2: The Color palette displaying the HSB color sliders

A-1:   Creating swatches

Here's how	Here's why
1 Start Adobe Photoshop CS3	Click Start and choose All Programs, Adobe Photoshop CS3.
On the Welcome Screen, click **Close**	If necessary.
Navigate to the current unit folder, and open Outlander logo	
Save the image as **My Outlander logo**	
2 Zoom in on the first **S** in "Spices"	Increase the size of the image window, press and hold Ctrl+Spacebar to access the Zoom tool, and drag across the "S" to zoom in on it.
Select the Eyedropper tool	
Click the **S**	To sample the color as the new foreground color.
3 Activate the Swatches palette	
Point to the blank area to the right of the last swatch, as shown	

The pointer changes to a paint can.

Click the mouse button	To add the foreground color as a swatch. The Color Swatch Name dialog box appears.
In the Name box, enter **Outlander orange**	
Click **OK**	To add the orange color to the Swatches palette.

4 In the Swatches palette, click as shown

To display the Swatches palette menu.

   Choose **Small List**

To display the swatches as a list.

   Scroll to the bottom of the list

To view the Outlander orange swatch.

You will separate the Swatches palette from the palette group so you can see the Swatches and Color palettes at the same time.

5 Drag the Swatches palette tab to the left

To separate the palette from its palette group.

   Drag the Swatches palette next to the palette group, as shown

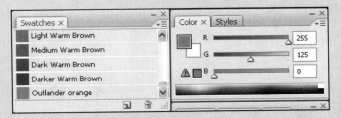

6 Activate the Color palette

If necessary.

   From the Color palette menu, choose **HSB Sliders**

To display the HSB color model's sliders. You'll use this color model to specify a slightly dimmer version of the color.

   Drag the B (Brightness) slider to **80**

To specify a dimmer color.

   In the Swatches palette, click 🔲

(The "Create new swatch of foreground color" button.) To add the adjusted color as a new swatch.

7 Double-click **Swatch 1**

To select the swatch name.

   Type **Darker orange** and press ⏎ ENTER

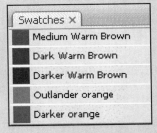

To rename the swatch. Next, you'll create a lighter version of the color.

8 In the Color palette, drag the B slider to **100**

Drag the S (Saturation) slider to **60**

To create a pale orange.

Press and hold (ALT) and click ⬛ in the Swatches palette

To add the swatch and automatically open the Color Swatch Name dialog box.

In the Name box, enter **Lighter orange**

Click **OK**

9 Create a color named **Very light orange**, with a Saturation value of **40**

In the Color palette, drag the S slider to 40. In the Swatches palette, Alt+click the "Create new swatch of foreground color" button. Enter "Very light orange" and click OK.

10 In the Swatches palette, click **Darker orange**

To select it as the foreground color

Press (CTRL) and click **Outlander orange**

To select it as the background color.

Press (ALT) and click **Very light orange**

To delete the swatch.

Fill shortcuts

Explanation

After you set a color as the foreground or background color, you can apply it by using a variety of techniques.

- To fill a selection on the Background layer with the background color, press Backspace or Delete. On other layers, pressing Backspace or Delete removes pixels, creating empty areas.

- To fill a selection with the foreground color, press Alt+Backspace or Alt+Delete.

- To fill a selection on any layer with the background color, press Ctrl+Backspace or Ctrl+Delete.

- To apply a fill with custom settings, choose Edit, Fill or press Shift+Backspace to open the Fill dialog box. From the Use list, select Foreground Color or Background Color, or select Color to open the Color Picker, from which you can select any color to use as the new fill. Under Blending, select a mode and an opacity for the color you're applying, as shown in Exhibit 1-3. Click OK.

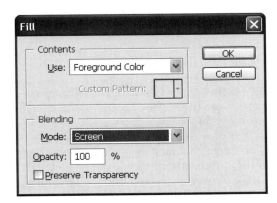

Exhibit 1-3: The Fill dialog box

When you use the Fill dialog box to specify a blending mode for the fill you're applying, the blending mode influences how the new fill will affect the existing colors on the current layer. The blending mode won't affect how the new fill interacts with colors on other layers.

Creating a file

When you choose File, New to create a Photoshop file, you can specify the image's dimensions, resolution, color mode, and background color. Rather than specifying values manually, you can choose from the Preset list to specify a standard size or other preset. The following table lists a few of the presets available.

Preset	Specifications
Default Photoshop Size	7" × 5" at 72ppi.
Clipboard	Uses the dimensions and resolution of the item currently on the Clipboard. This is useful when you've cut or copied content that you want to paste into a new Photoshop file.
U.S. Paper	8.5" × 11" at 300 ppi.
Photo	3" × 2" at 300 ppi.
Web	640 pixels × 480 pixels at 72 ppi.
Mobile & Devices	176 pixels × 208 pixels at 72 ppi.
Film & Video	720 pixels × 480 pixels at 72 ppi, with a pixel aspect ratio of 0.9. This matches the frame size of NTSC video, commonly used for TV broadcasts in the United States.
	Unlike computer monitors, which display square pixels, televisions display pixels that are narrower than they are tall. If you view a 720px × 480px image on a computer monitor with square pixels, the image looks wider than it would on TV. When you specify a pixel aspect ratio of 0.9 to match that of TV, Photoshop displays the image within the space of 648 × 480 pixels, approximating its appearance on TV.
	You can change the pixel aspect ratio of any image by using the Image, Pixel Aspect Ratio submenu, and turn the correction on or off with the View, Pixel Aspect Ratio Correction command.
<open image name>	Any open images are listed at the bottom of the Preset list. You can select an open image to use its settings for the image you're creating.

Do it!

A-2: Filling selections

Here's how	Here's why
1 Choose **File**, **New...**	To open the New dialog box.
In the Name box, enter **Background ideas**	
2 Observe the Preset value	The preset value is set to Default Photoshop Size.
3 From the Width list, select **pixels**	(If necessary.) To set both the width and the height to pixels.
In the Width box, enter **600**	
In the Height box, enter **600**	
In the Resolution box, enter **300**	

New
Name: Background ideas
Preset: Custom
Size:
Width: 600   pixels
Height: 600   pixels
Resolution: 300   pixels/inch
Color Mode: RGB Color   8 bit
Background Contents: White

4 Observe the Preset value	Because you specified custom settings, the Preset value automatically changed to "Custom."
Click **OK**	To create the new document.
5 Press (CTRL) + (A)	To select all pixels on the Background layer.
Press (← BACKSPACE)	To fill the image with the current background color.

6 Create a layer called **Circles**

Press Alt and click the "Create a new layer" button in the Layers palette. Enter "Circles" in the Name box, and click OK.

Deselect the image

Press Ctrl+D.

Create a selection in the shape of a circle

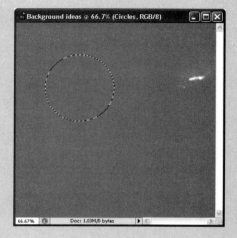

Use the Elliptical Marquee tool while pressing Shift to create a perfect circle.

7 In the Swatches palette, click **Lighter orange**

To set the current foreground color to Lighter orange.

Press ⟮ ALT ⟯ + ⟮ ← BACKSPACE ⟯

To fill the selected marquee with the Lighter orange color. (Because this is not the Background layer, pressing Backspace by itself would have deleted the selected pixels.)

Deselect the image

Press Ctrl+D.

8 Make a smaller circular selection inside the first circle, as shown

9 Press (CTRL) and click **Darker orange**	To set that color as the background color.
	You will use both the Lighter orange and Darker orange colors repeatedly, so you want them to be available in the toolbox.
Press (← BACKSPACE)	To delete the pixels from the Circles layer.
	Unlike on the Background layer, pressing Backspace on any other layer does not fill the selection with the background color. Instead, pressing Backspace removes the pixels and creates a transparent area within the selection.
Hide, and then show, the Background layer	(In the Layers palette, click the eye icon next to the Background layer.) To view the transparent space.
10 Select the **Circles** layer	If necessary.
Press (CTRL) + (← BACKSPACE)	To fill the selection with the background color.
Deselect the image	
11 On the Circles layer, draw an overlapping circular marquee, as shown	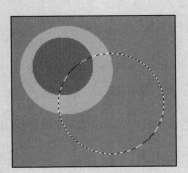
Verify that Lighter orange is the current foreground color	
12 Press (SHIFT) + (← BACKSPACE)	To open the Fill dialog box. You'll use a blending mode to create a semi-transparent effect.
From the Use list, select **Foreground Color**	(If necessary.) To select the Lighter orange color.
From the Mode list, select **Screen**	To make the fill color lighten the colors it overlaps.

13 Click **OK**

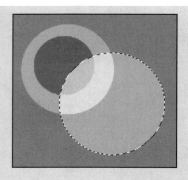

To fill the circle. The blending mode lightened the two circles where the new circle overlaps them. The blending mode had no effect on the orange color in the background, however, because it's on a different layer.

Deselect the circle

14 Create another circular selection, as shown

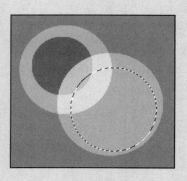

Open the Fill dialog box

Press Shift+Backspace.

From the Mode list, select **Multiply**

Click **OK**

To fill the circle.

15 Deselect the circle

16 Choose **File**, **Save**

To open the Save As dialog box. The name you specified earlier appears in the File name box.

Navigate to the current unit folder and click **Save**

Fill layers

Explanation

Another way to add a color to an image is to create a fill layer. A fill layer can contain a solid color, a gradient, or a pattern.

Using a fill layer to apply a fill requires fewer steps than does creating a blank layer and then filling it. In addition, you might want to use a fill layer to apply a solid color, a gradient, or a pattern because if you later change the image's canvas size, the fill layer expands to fill the new space.

To create a fill layer:

1 Open the dialog box for the type of fill layer you want to create. Do either of the following:

- At the bottom of the Layers palette, click the "Create new fill or adjustment layer" icon, and choose Solid Color, Gradient, or Pattern to open the appropriate dialog box.
- Choose Layer, New Fill Layer and choose Solid Color, Gradient, or Pattern to open the New Layer dialog box. Specify the layer name, and click OK to open the appropriate dialog box for the type of fill layer you chose.

2 Specify the settings you want.

3 Click OK.

Another benefit of using a fill layer is that you can easily change its settings by double-clicking the fill layer's thumbnail, shown in Exhibit 1-4, to open a dialog box.

- Double-click a solid-color fill layer's icon to open the Color Picker dialog box.
- Double-click a gradient fill layer's icon to open the Gradient Fill dialog box.
- Double-click a pattern fill layer's icon to open the Pattern Fill dialog box.

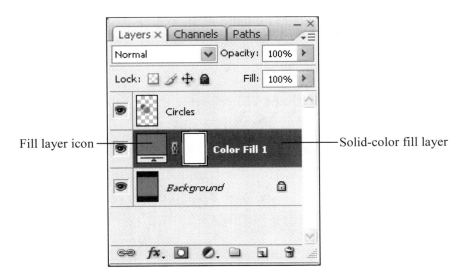

Exhibit 1-4: A solid-color fill layer in the Layers palette

A-3: Creating fill layers

Here's how	Here's why
1 Press ⓓ	To return the foreground and background colors to their defaults.
2 Choose **Image**, **Canvas Size...**	To open the Canvas Size dialog box. You'll add one inch to the height of the canvas.
In the Height box, enter **3**	
Verify that Relative is cleared	
Verify that Background is selected in the Canvas extension color list	
Click **OK**	The image canvas extends an additional inch, but the additional canvas is white (the current background color).
Choose **Edit**, **Undo Canvas Size**	You'll create a fill layer with the background color to see what happens when you resize the canvas.
3 Choose **Layer**, **New Fill Layer**, **Solid Color...**	To open the New Layer dialog box.
Click **OK**	The Color Picker dialog box appears.
In the Swatches palette, click **Outlander orange**	
Click **OK**	
4 Move the **Color Fill 1** layer below the Circles layer	(In the Layers palette.) You'll once again add to the canvas size to see the result of the fill layer.
5 Choose **Image**, **Canvas Size...**	To open the Canvas Size dialog box.
In the Height box, enter **3**	
Verify that Relative is cleared	
Click **OK**	The fill layer expands automatically as the canvas expands.
6 Update the file	

Topic B: Gradients and patterns

This topic covers the following Adobe ACE exam objectives for Photoshop CS3.

#	Objective
1.2	Given a scenario, create a tool preset.
2.5	Create and use gradients and patterns.

Gradients

Explanation

A *gradient* is a blend of two or more colors, in which the colors fade gradually from one to another. You can use the Gradient tool to drag within a layer or selection to specify the angle and length of a gradient.

To create a gradient with the Gradient tool:

1   In the toolbox, select the Gradient tool.

2   On the options bar, click the Gradient Picker arrow to open the Gradient Picker. Select the gradient you want, or choose New Gradient from the Gradient Picker menu to create a custom gradient. Then, close the Gradient Picker.

3   On the options bar, click the icon for the gradient type you want to use: Linear, Radial, Angle, Reflected, or Diamond.

The gradient type determines how the colors are arranged. For example, a linear gradient displays colors blending from one to another in a straight line. A radial gradient displays one color at the center and blends outward to the other colors.

4   Drag across the image or selection to specify the angle and length of the gradient. The distance you drag the Gradient tool specifies the gradient's *blend area:* where the colors blend together. If you drag across only part of the layer or selection, then the area outside that region is filled with the gradient's beginning or ending colors.

5   To modify the gradient's colors and other settings, click the gradient sample on the options bar; this opens the Gradient Editor dialog box, shown in Exhibit 1-5. If you want to create a new gradient preset, enter a name and click New. Click OK to finish editing the gradient.

The following table describes some of the settings in the Gradient Editor dialog box.

Item	Description
Palette menu	Select a different set of gradients, or change how the gradient list is displayed.
Presets	Click a gradient to view and change its settings. If you change its settings, its name changes to "Custom" so that your changes don't affect the original gradient.
Name box	Enter a name for the gradient.
Color stop	Click a color stop to select it so you can change its color. To move a color stop, you can drag it or type a new position in the Location box. To add a color stop, click below the gradient bar. To remove a color stop, drag it away from the gradient bar. (A gradient must have at least two color stops, so you can't remove the last two.)
Opacity stop	Click an opacity stop to select it so you can change the opacity setting at that location. To move an opacity stop, you can drag it or type a new position in the Location box. To add an opacity stop, click above the gradient bar. To remove a stop, drag it away from the gradient bar.
Midpoint	When you click a color stop or opacity stop, a diamond appears between it and the next stop. The diamond represents the blending midpoint between the two stops. To adjust the midpoint, either drag it or type a new value in the Location box.

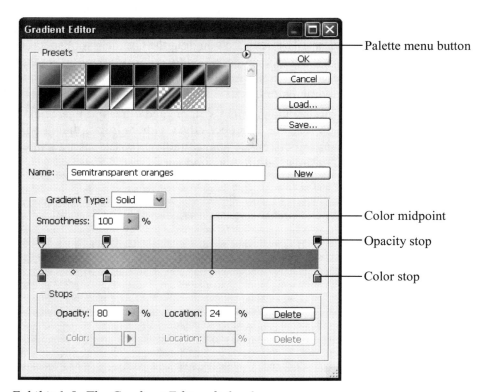

Exhibit 1-5: The Gradient Editor dialog box

Gradient fill layers

You can apply a gradient to an entire layer by creating a gradient fill layer. To create a gradient fill layer:

1   In the Layers palette, click the "Create new fill or adjustment layer" icon, and choose Gradient to open the Gradient Fill dialog box, shown in Exhibit 1-6.

2   Specify the options you want.

3   Click OK.

4   If you want to modify the gradient fill layer, double-click its icon to open the Gradient Fill dialog box. Specify the desired settings and click OK.

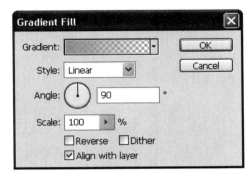

Exhibit 1-6: The Gradient Fill dialog box

B-1: Creating gradients

Here's how	Here's why
1 Choose **View**, **Fit on Screen**	To display the entire image in the window.
2 Select the **Circles** layer	In the Layers palette.
3 Set the foreground color to **Lighter orange**	In the Swatches palette, click Lighter orange.
Set the background color to **Darker orange**	In the Swatches palette, press Ctrl and click Darker orange.
4 Create a layer named **Fade**	
Place the layer below the Circles layer	
5 In the toolbox, click	The Gradient tool.
Display the Gradient Picker	Click the Gradient Picker drop-down arrow on the options bar.
Verify that the first gradient in the Gradient Picker is selected	
	The Foreground to Background gradient.
Close the Gradient Picker	Click the Gradient Picker drop-down arrow.
6 Drag from the top-left corner of the image to the bottom-right corner	To create the gradient.

7 Observe the image

The gradient goes from the top-left corner to the bottom-right corner.

Next, you'll create a new gradient and apply it to another layer.

8 On the options bar, click the gradient sample

To open the Gradient Editor dialog box. You'll create a gradient that includes three defined colors.

Click the left color stop, as shown

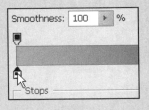

To select the foreground color stop.

9 In the Swatches palette, click **Darker orange**

To apply the color as the foreground color for the gradient.

Click the right color stop, as shown

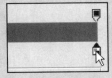

To select the background color stop.

Set the color to **Outlander orange**

In the Swatches palette, click Outlander orange.

10 Click below the gradient bar, as shown

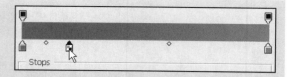

To create another color stop.

Set the color for the stop to **Lighter orange**

You'll drag the color midpoint diamonds closer to the center gradient stop to narrow the Lighter orange portion of the gradient.

Drag the color midpoint diamonds closer to the center color stop, as shown

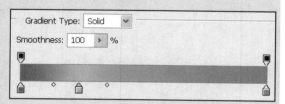

To make the Lighter orange portion of the gradient narrower.

Next, you'll reduce the opacity for the gradient at the center stop.

Click above the gradient bar, as shown

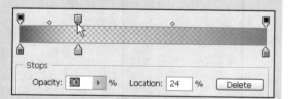

To create an opacity stop above the center color stop.

Under Stops, set the Opacity value to **80**

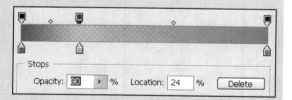

To create a slightly transparent area of the gradient.

11 In the Name box, enter **Semitransparent oranges**

Click **New**

To save the custom gradient.

Click **OK**

12 Above all of the other layers, create a layer named **Highlight**

13 In the Highlight layer, use the Semitransparent oranges gradient to create a linear gradient, extending from the top-right corner to the bottom-left corner of the image

14 Observe the image

Drag from the top-right corner to the bottom-left corner.

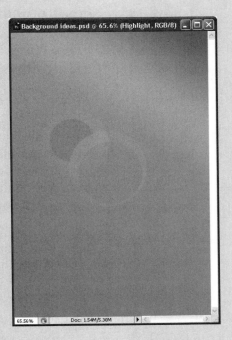

Because the new gradient is semi-transparent, you can see through it to the circles you created on the layer below.

15 Update the file

Patterns

Explanation
In addition to using solid colors and gradients, you can fill a layer or selection with a pattern. A *pattern* is a rectangular image area that repeats to fill a layer or selection. You can apply one of the patterns that comes with Photoshop, or you can create your own patterns.

To create a custom pattern:

1 Use the Rectangular Marquee tool to select the image area you want to define as a pattern. The selection must use a Feather value of zero.
2 Choose Edit, Define Pattern to open the Pattern Name dialog box.
3 In the Name box, enter a name for the pattern.
4 Click OK.

To apply a pattern to a layer or an image area:

1 In the Layers palette, click the layer you want to fill with the pattern, or use a selection tool to select the area you want to fill. If there is no selection, the pattern will fill the entire layer.
2 Press Shift+Backspace or choose Edit, Fill to open the Fill dialog box.
3 From the Use list, select Pattern.
4 From the Custom Pattern list, select the pattern you want to use. You can use the Custom Pattern palette menu to change how the patterns are displayed in the list or to select a different set of patterns.
5 Under Blending, specify any blending options you want to use.
6 Click OK.

Rectangular Marquee tool options

Before you select an area you want to define as a custom pattern, you can set Rectangular Marquee tool options to help you make the selection you want. For example, you can specify that the Rectangular Marquee tool select areas by using a specific aspect ratio or specific dimensions.

To specify an aspect ratio or dimensions for the Rectangular Marquee tool:

1 Select the Rectangular Marquee tool.
2 On the options bar, select Fixed Ratio or Fixed Size from the Style list.
3 In the Width and Height boxes, enter the ratio or dimensions you want to use.

Pattern fill layers

You can also add a pattern to an image by using a pattern fill layer. To create a pattern fill layer:

1 In the Layers palette, click the "Create new fill or adjustment layer" icon and choose Pattern to open the Pattern Fill dialog box.
2 Specify the options you want.
3 Click OK.
4 If you want to modify the pattern fill layer, double-click its icon to open the Pattern Fill dialog box. Specify the desired settings and click OK.

Do it!

B-2: Creating a simple pattern

Here's how	Here's why
1 Choose **Window**, **My outlander logo**	
Choose **View**, **Fit on Screen**	If necessary, to display the entire image.
2 Select the Rectangular Marquee tool	
On the options bar, from the Style list, select **Fixed Size**	
In the Width box, enter **160 px**	
In the Height box, enter **160 px**	To set the marquee to a fixed size and a square shape.
3 Click in the image	To place the marquee. Because the marquee was set to a fixed size, you didn't need to drag to create it.
Drag inside the image to position the marquee as shown	
4 Choose **Edit**, **Define Pattern...**	To open the Pattern Name dialog box.
In the Name box, enter **Chiles**	
Click **OK**	To create the pattern.
5 Activate the Background ideas image	Choose Window, Background ideas.
Create a layer named **Chiles**	
Place the Chiles layer above the other layers	If necessary.

6 Press (SHIFT) + (← BACKSPACE)   To open the Fill dialog box.

From the Use list, select **Pattern**

From the Custom Pattern list, select the Chiles pattern

From the Mode list, select **Normal**

Click **OK**

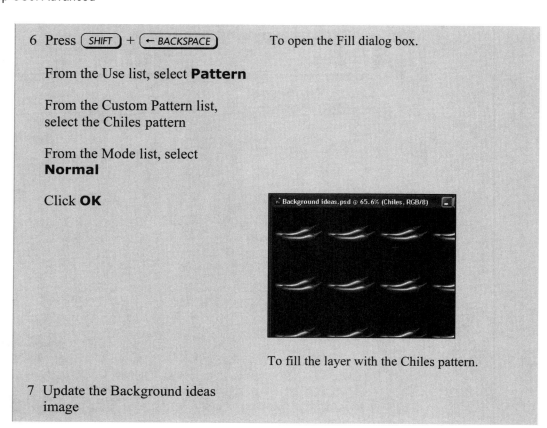

To fill the layer with the Chiles pattern.

7 Update the Background ideas image

Offset patterns

Explanation   Instead of creating a pattern in which a repeating item appears in columns and rows, you can create an offset pattern, as shown in Exhibit 1-7.

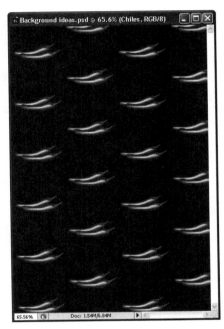

Exhibit 1-7: An offset pattern

To create an offset pattern:

1   Create a pattern using the item that you want to display as an offset pattern.
2   Create a new image that is twice the height and width of a single tile of the pattern you created.
3   Fill the image with the pattern, which will tile four times in the image, with two vertical tiles and two horizontal tiles.
4   Make a selection that includes two vertical tiles of the pattern (the entire image height and half its width).
5   Choose Filter, Other, Offset. Specify a vertical offset value that is half the height of a single pattern tile, and click OK. The two tiles you selected and offset are now offset from the other two tiles in the image.
6   Select the entire image, and create a new pattern. When you fill an image with the new pattern, it will appear as an offset pattern, as shown in Exhibit 1-7.

The Pattern Maker

You can also create abstract patterns based on colors in a rectangular selection by choosing Filter, Pattern Maker. You can then click Generate to preview the image with the filter applied, and click OK to apply the filter to the image.

Do it! **B-3: Creating an offset pattern**

Here's how	Here's why
1 Choose **File, New...**	To open the New dialog box. You'll create a temporary image that you will use to create an offset pattern.
Name the image **Chiles offset**	
Set the image size to **320 pixels** by **320 pixels** with a resolution of **300**	You're setting the size of the image to twice the height and width of the pattern you will use.
Set the Color Mode value to **RGB Color**	If necessary.
Click **OK**	To create the image.
2 Press (SHIFT) + (← BACKSPACE)	To open the Fill dialog box.
Verify that Pattern appears in the Use box, and that the Chiles pattern is selected in the Custom Pattern list	Contents Use: Pattern Custom Pattern:
Click **OK**	Chiles offset @ 100% (RGB/8)
	To apply the pattern background to the image.

3 Select the Rectangular Marquee tool

If necessary.

On the options bar, in the Height box, enter **320 px**

Click to place the marquee, and then drag it to the right side of the image, as shown

The marquee width is still set to 160 px, which is half the width of the image.

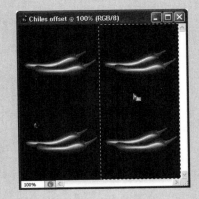

You will now use the Offset filter to move the selected area in the image.

4 Choose **Filter, Other, Offset...**

To open the Offset dialog box.

In the Vertical box, enter **80**

Under Undefined Areas, verify that Wrap Around is selected

Click **OK**

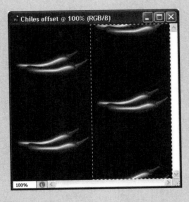

To create the offset in the pattern.

5 Press (CTRL) + (A)

To select the entire image area.

Using the selected area, define a pattern called **Chiles offset**

(Choose Edit, Define Pattern and click OK.) The pattern name will already appear in the Name box in the Pattern Name dialog box because that is the name of the image.

6 Activate the Background Ideas image

With the Chiles layer selected, press CTRL + A | To select the entire image area.

Open the Fill dialog box | Press Shift+Backspace.

From the Custom Pattern list, select the Chiles offset pattern | The Chiles offset pattern is half the height of the original Chiles pattern because Photoshop automatically determined that the lower half of the pattern is a copy of the upper half, and only the top portion is needed to define the pattern.

Click **OK** | To apply the Chiles offset pattern, as shown in Exhibit 1-7.

7 Update the Background ideas image

8 Activate the Chiles offset image | You no longer need this image now that you've used it to define the new pattern.

Close Chiles offset without saving it

The Preset Manager

Explanation

Each swatch, gradient, or pattern in Photoshop is called a *preset*. Brushes, styles, contours, custom shapes, and tool settings are also stored as presets. Presets include both those you create and those supplied with Photoshop.

You can use the Preset Manager dialog box, shown in Exhibit 1-8, to load presets that come with Photoshop. You can also use the Preset Manager dialog box to save a group of presets you've created or edited. The group will be saved as a file called a *set*. Sets can be useful for a few reasons:

- You can share sets of presets with other people for consistency.
- You can create multiple preset files that you can load for different purposes. For example, a freelance designer could save different color palettes for different clients.
- If you need to reinstall Photoshop, you can reload the presets you saved instead of losing them.

To manage presets and sets:

1 Choose Edit, Preset Manager (or choose Preset Manager from a palette menu).

2 From the Preset Type list, select one of the eight preset types.

3 Select the presets you want to work with. Shift+click to select a range of adjacent presets, and Ctrl+click to select non-adjacent ones.

4 Click Save Set to save the selected presets as a set. If you save the set in the default location (a subfolder of the Presets folder within the Photoshop application folder), then, after you close and re-open Photoshop, the set will appear in the palette menu, along with sets that came with Photoshop.

5 Select options from the Preset Manager list to change the display, to reset or replace presets, or to select a set from the ones listed.

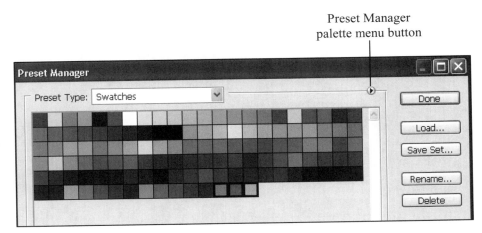

Exhibit 1-8: The Preset Manager dialog box

Do it!

B-4: Saving a set of presets

Here's how	Here's why
1 Choose **Edit**, **Preset Manager...**	To open the Preset Manager dialog box. You'll save, as a set, the three colors you added to the Swatches palette earlier.
2 From the Preset Type list, select **Swatches**	
3 Scroll to the bottom of the swatches	(If necessary.) To display the colors you added.
4 Point to the swatch that's third from the last, and notice the name that appears	To verify that the swatch is named Outlander Orange.
5 Click the Outlander Orange swatch	
Hold (SHIFT) and click the last swatch	To select the range of three adjacent swatches you created, as shown in Exhibit 1-8.
6 Click **Save Set**	To open the Save dialog box.
In the File name box, enter **Outlander oranges**	
Verify that the Color Swatches folder is selected in the Save in list	To ensure that the set will be saved alongside the swatch sets that come with Photoshop.
Click **Save**	To save the set. You can now delete these swatches and reload them later if necessary.
7 Click **Delete**	To delete the swatch presets you created.
Click **Done**	To make the Outlander oranges set appear in the Preset Manager palette menu, you need to close and re-open Photoshop.
8 Close Photoshop, updating files as prompted	
Start Photoshop	
9 From the Swatches palette menu, choose **Preset Manager...**	To open the Preset Manager dialog box with Swatches selected so you can re-load the set you created.

10 From the Preset Manager palette menu, choose **Outlander oranges**

To add those colors to the swatches. A new Preset Manager dialog box appears, asking if you want to replace the existing swatches or append the new ones.

Click **Append**

To add the colors to the existing ones.

Click **Done**

Tool presets

A tool preset is one of the eight categories of presets. You can use tool presets to save and reuse specified settings for a particular tool.

To create a tool preset:

1   Select the tool for which you want to create a preset.
2   On the options bar, specify the tool settings you want to store.
3   Do either of the following to open the New Tool Preset dialog box:
    - On the left side of the options bar, click the Tool Preset button to display the Tool Preset Picker, and click the "Create new tool preset" button.
    - Choose Window, Tool Presets to open the Tool Presets palette, and click the "Create new tool preset" button.
4   In the New Tool Preset dialog box, enter a name for the tool preset and click OK.

After saving a tool preset, you can select it by choosing it from the Tool Preset picker or from the Tool Presets palette. If you want to reset the current tool to its default settings, right-click the tool on the options bar and choose Reset Tool.

B-5:   Creating a tool preset

Here's how	Here's why
1 Select the Rectangular Marquee tool	(If necessary.) You'll create two presets for this tool, representing two sets of dimensions for selection marquees that you'll use often in your work.
2 From the Style list, verify that Fixed Size is selected	(On the options bar.) You'll create a preset for square selections that are 90 pixels wide and tall.
In the Width and Height boxes, enter **90 px**	
3 Click as shown to display the Tool Preset picker	

4 Click the "Create new tool preset" button, as shown

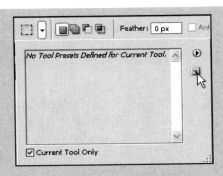

To open the New Tool Preset dialog box.

5 Edit the Name box to read **Rectangular Marquee 90 px**

Click **OK**

To save the tool preset. The options bar displays the settings you specified.

You'll create a second preset that specifies a 45-pixel width and a 5-pixel feather for selections.

6 In the Width box, enter **45 px**

On the options bar.

In the Feather box, enter **5 px**

Save the current settings as a preset named **Rectangular Marquee 45x90 px, 5 px Feather**

Display the Tool Preset picker and click the "Create new tool preset" button. In the New Tool Preset dialog box, enter "Rectangular Marquee 45x90 px, 5 px Feather" and click OK.

You can now switch among these two presets.

7 Choose **Window, Tool Presets**

To open the Tool Presets palette.

8 Observe the list of presets in the palette

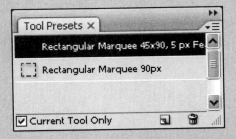

The two tool presets you just created appear in the palette.

9 Click the **Rectangular Marquee 90 px** preset

(In the Tool Presets palette.) To select the preset.

Observe the options bar settings

The options bar displays the preset's settings.

10 Open the Background ideas image

In the current unit folder.

11 Click within the image	To generate a selection based on the current settings.
Press (CTRL) + (D)	To deselect the image.
12 Click the **Rectangular Marquee 45x90 px, 5 px Feather** preset	(In the Tool Presets palette.) To select the preset. The options bar displays this preset's settings.
13 Click within the image	To generate a selection based on this preset's settings.
14 Deselect the image	
15 Close the Tool Presets palette	You'll return the Rectangular Marquee tool to its default preset settings.
16 On the options bar, right-click the Rectangular Marquee tool as shown	To display a shortcut menu.
Choose **Reset Tool**	The Rectangular Marquee tool settings on the options bar return to the default settings. However, the two tool presets you created are still available for you to select at any time.

Topic C: Layer overlays

This topic covers the following Adobe ACE exam objective for Photoshop CS3.

#	Objective
2.5	Create and use gradients and patterns.

Overlay layer styles

Explanation

Another way to apply a fill, gradient, or pattern to a layer is to use an overlay layer style. An *overlay layer style* applies a fill, gradient, or pattern to only the existing pixels in a layer, similar to using a layer clipping mask.

Gradient overlays

The Gradient Overlay layer style fills the existing layer content with the gradient you specify. This layer style is particularly useful for applying a gradient to text. Even after applying a gradient overlay, you can continue to edit and format the text.

By default, a gradient overlay aligns with the layer content. Therefore, if you change the text on a type layer or paint additional areas on a layer, the gradient adjusts to automatically flow across the new layer content.

To specify settings for the gradient overlay, select Gradient Overlay in the list of styles in the Layer Style dialog box. The Gradient Overlay style options are shown in Exhibit 1-9.

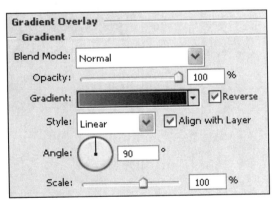

Exhibit 1-9: The Gradient Overlay options in the Layer Style dialog box

To create an overlay layer style:
1 Double-click the layer thumbnail or the space to the right of the layer name to open the Layer Style dialog box.
2 In the list of styles, select the type of overlay you want to use: Color Overlay, Gradient Overlay, or Pattern Overlay.
3 Specify the options you want to use, such as transparency.
4 For gradient and pattern overlays, point to the image and drag to reposition the gradient or pattern relative to the layer content through which it appears. This works only while the Layer Style dialog box is open.
5 Click OK.

Do it!

C-1: Filling areas with overlay layer styles

Here's how	Here's why
1 Double-click the Chiles layer	To open the Layer Style dialog box. You'll dim the chiles in the pattern to make it more subdued.
Under Styles, click **Color Overlay**	(Click the words themselves, not the check box to their left.) To check the check box and display the Color Overlay settings.
Click the color swatch next to the Blend Mode list, as shown	

Color Overlay
Color
Blend Mode: Normal
Opacity: 100 %

To open the Select overlay color dialog box.

In the R, G, and B boxes, enter **0**

Select overlay color:

new

current

H: 0 °
S: 0 %
B: 0 %
R: 0
G: 0
B: 0

Only Web Colors

To specify a black color.

| 2 Click **OK** | To select the black color for the overlay. |
| Set the Opacity value to **80%** | |

Color Overlay
Color
Blend Mode: Normal
Opacity: 80 %

| Click **OK** | To create a dimmed pattern. Next you'll add some text. |
| 3 Hide the Chiles layer | So you'll be able to see the text more clearly as you add it. |

4 In the toolbox, click **T**.   The Horizontal Type tool.

   On the options bar, set the font to
   Impact

   Set the font size to **30 pt**

   Click to place the insertion point
   near the left edge of the image

   Type **Hot stuff!**   To create a type layer.

   Use the Move tool to center the
   text on the image

5 In the Layers palette, double-click   To open the Layer Style dialog box.
   the Hot Stuff! layer

   Click **Gradient Overlay**   To display the Gradient Overlay settings.

   From the Gradient list, select
   Violet, Orange as indicated

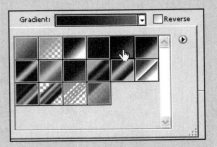

   Check **Reverse**   To reverse the gradient colors.

   Click **OK**   To apply the gradient overlay to the type layer.

6 Show the Chiles layer

7 Using the Move tool, drag the text anywhere in the image

To observe that the gradient stays fixed relative to the text.

In the Hot Stuff! layer, click the arrow to the right of [fx]

(If necessary.) To view the layer styles applied.

Double-click **Gradient Overlay**

To open the Layer Style dialog box.

Clear **Align with Layer**

Click **OK**

Using the Move tool, drag the text anywhere in the image

Observe that the colors in the text change as you move it; this occurs because the gradient now applies to the whole image.

Next, you'll align the gradient with the layer content.

8 Double-click **Gradient Overlay**

In the Layers palette.

Check **Align with Layer**

With the dialog box still open, you'll drag the image to move the gradient within the text.

Point to the image and drag up slowly

To display less of the violet color.

9 Click **OK**

To close the Layer Style dialog box.

10 Update and close the image

Unit summary: Fills and overlays

Topic A   In this topic, you added colors to the **Swatches palette** and used fill shortcuts to fill selections and layers with color. In addition, you used **fill layers** to create layers filled with solid color.

Topic B   In this topic, you learned how to use the Gradient tool to add a **gradient fill** to a layer or selection. In addition, you learned how to create a **gradient fill layer** to add a gradient to an image. You also created and applied **patterns** and offset patterns. Finally, you used the Preset Manager to save a set of color swatches as a **preset** and to save tool presets.

Topic C   In this topic, you learned how to use **overlay layer styles** to fill layer content with a color, gradient, or pattern.

Independent practice activity

In this activity, you'll create custom swatches and save them as a set. You'll also apply fills, create a pattern, and create an offset pattern. Finally, you'll create a fill layer and apply an overlay layer style.

1 Open Practice outlander logo, located in the current unit folder. Save the image as **My practice outlander logo**.

2 Create three swatches by sampling colors from the chile pepper. Sample a dark red color, a light red color, and a dark green color, and name the new colors **Chile dark red**, **Chile light red**, and **Chile dark green**.

3 Save the three colors as a set named **Chile colors**.

4 Create an image named **Triangles** that's 5"×5" at 300ppi, in RGB color mode. Set the foreground color to Chile dark red, and set the background color to Chile dark green. (*Hint:* Click Chile dark red to set it as the foreground color, and Ctrl+click Chile dark green to set it as the background color.)

5 On a new blank layer, create a triangular selection with the Polygonal Lasso tool, as shown in Exhibit 1-10. Fill the selection with the foreground color. Create another triangle that overlaps the first one, and fill it with the background color, using the Screen blending mode.

  To make horizontal or vertical lines with the Polygonal Lasso, click Shift while selecting points. To fill the first triangle, press Alt+Backspace or Alt+Delete. To fill the second triangle, choose Edit, Fill or press Shift+Backspace to open the Fill dialog box. Here you can apply the current background color with the Screen blending mode.

6 If you have time, create additional overlapping triangular selections, filling them with the colors you defined and using blending modes to create a geometric design.

7 Switch to My practice outlander logo.

8 Create a simple pattern using the word **Outlander** from the logo. Make the dimension of the tiles 600 pixels wide by 160 pixels tall.

  To do this step, select the Rectangular Marquee tool. Enter the width and height in the boxes on the options bar. Click the word "Outlander" to select it. Choose Edit, Define Pattern, and give the new pattern a name.

9 Create an offset pattern using the simple pattern you just created.

To do this step, create an image that's twice the height and width of the tile selected in My practice outlander logo. Fill the new image with the pattern you created. Be sure to set the Blending mode back to Normal. In the Height box on the options bar, enter 320 px. Select the right half of the image; choose Filter, Other, Offset; and enter a vertical offset value of 80 pixels. Select the entire image. Apply the Define Pattern command to define the image as a new pattern.

10 Create an image named **Offset logo** that's 600×600 pixels at 300ppi and uses RGB color mode. Create a fill layer with a solid red color (Chile light red). (*Hint*: Click the "Create new fill or adjustment layer" icon and choose Solid Color to open the Color Picker. Click the Chile light red swatch in the Swatches palette and click OK.)

11 Place the Outlander offset pattern into the image, using a Pattern Overlay layer style at 20% opacity. In addition, use Lighten mode and apply a 30% scale, as shown in Exhibit 1-11.

To do this step, press Ctrl+A to select the entire area. Double-click the layer thumbnail or the space to the right of the layer name to open the Layer Style dialog box. Select Pattern Overlay from the Styles list, and select the new offset pattern from the Pattern list. Change the other settings as described, and click OK.

12 Observe the offset pattern, which should appear similar to Exhibit 1-12.

13 Save and close all images.

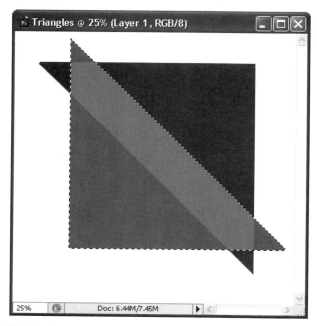

Exhibit 1-10: The two triangles as they appear after Step 5 in the independent practice activity

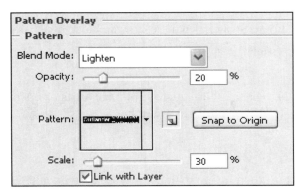

Exhibit 1-11: The Pattern Overlay layer-style settings as described in Step 11

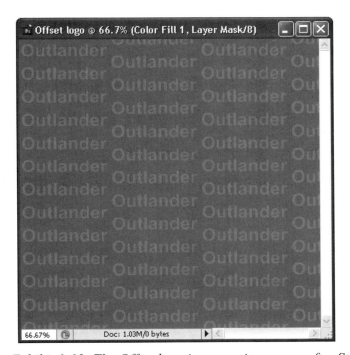

Exhibit 1-12: The Offset logo image as it appears after Step 11

Review questions

1 True or false: In the Swatches palette, a swatch can consist of a color, a pattern, or a gradient.

2 When you use keyboard shortcuts to fill image areas or open the Fill dialog box, you use the Alt, Ctrl, or Shift keys and the _____ key.

3 How would you fill an image with color that automatically expands if you enlarge the canvas size?

4 After specifying tool settings on the options bar, how can you save those settings as a tool preset? [Choose all that apply.]

   A On the options bar, right-click the tool's icon and choose Reset Tool.

   B Click the Tool Preset button to display the Tool Preset Picker, and click the "Create new tool preset" button.

   C Choose Window, Tool Presets to open the Tool Presets palette, and click the "Create new tool preset" button.

   D Select an option from the list of presets in the Tool Preset Picker.

5 You want to add a gradient on the current layer. Which technique should you use?

   A Choose Layer, New Fill Layer, Gradient.

   B In the Layers palette, click the "Create new fill or adjustment layer" icon and choose Gradient.

   C Select the Gradient tool, select a gradient from the Gradient Picker, and drag in the image.

   D Select a gradient swatch in the Swatches palette, and then press Alt+Delete to fill the layer with that gradient.

6 Of the following statements about the selected area you use to define a pattern, which one is true?

   A The selection must be perfectly square.

   B The selection must be rectangular.

   C The selection can be any shape.

   D The selection can have any feather value.

7 After you specify a selection that you want to define as a pattern, which technique should you use to define the pattern?

   A Choose Layer, New Fill Layer, Pattern.

   B Choose Edit, Define Pattern.

   C In the Layers palette, click the "Create new fill or adjustment layer" icon and choose Pattern.

   D Choose Edit, Fill.

8 You've added several new colors to the Swatches palette. Which command can you use to save them as a file that you can load at any time or share with others?

   A Edit, Preset Manager

   B Select, Save Selection

   C Layer, New Fill Layer, Solid Color

   D Image, Adjustments, Replace Color

9 For what purposes might you use the Preset Manager dialog box? [Choose all that apply.]

   A To reset all Photoshop preferences.

   B To save the current palette locations so you can return to that palette arrangement at any time.

   C To load a set of brushes for use with the Brush tool.

   D To export a set of custom tool presets as a file so you can load the tool presets on a coworker's computer.

10 To create a gradient that automatically aligns with a type layer's contents even when you edit the text, what should you use?

11 What dialog box do overlays appear in?

Unit 2

Masks

Unit time: 50 minutes

Complete this unit, and you'll know how to:

A Paint in Quick Mask mode and in an alpha channel to specify a selection.

B Create a layer mask to hide part of a layer.

C Create grayscale masks to partially mask part of an image.

D Use a clipping mask to conform one layer to the shape of another.

Topic A: Mask channels

This topic covers the following Adobe ACE exam objective for Photoshop CS3.

#	Objective
4.4	Create and modify selections by using the Channels palette.

Using masks

Explanation

When you select part of an image, the areas outside the selection are *masked*, because you can't paint in those areas. This concept is similar to having a painter use masking tape to cover areas that should not be painted.

In addition to using Photoshop's selection tools to select image areas, you can use painting tools to do the same thing. The painting tools can be more intuitive than the selection tools and can make it easier to add to or subtract from a complex selection. To specify image selections by painting, you can paint in Quick Mask mode or in an alpha channel.

Quick Masks

One way to create a selection by painting is to use *Quick Mask mode*. This mode displays a semi-transparent colored overlay to differentiate between selected and non-selected areas. By default, the color appears over all image areas that are not selected (the masked areas), although you can reverse this. In Quick Mask mode, you can use the painting tools to add to or subtract from the selection. In the default configuration, painting with black adds to the masked area, and painting with white adds to the selected area.

To activate Quick Mask mode, click the toolbox's Edit in Quick Mask Mode button or press Q. To return to Standard mode (in which a selection appears as a marquee), click the Edit in Standard Mode button or press Q.

By default, the masking color is red. If that's hard to distinguish from the image, you can change the masking color.

To change the masking color:

1 Double-click the Edit in Quick Mask Mode button to open the Quick Mask Options dialog box, shown in Exhibit 2-1.

2 Under Color, click the color swatch to open the Select Quick Mask color dialog box.

3 Specify the color you want to use. Click OK to return to the Quick Mask Options dialog box.

4 Under Color, adjust the Opacity value, if necessary.

5 Click OK.

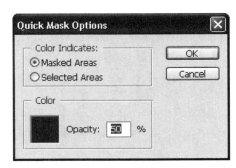

Exhibit 2-1: The Quick Mask Options dialog box

Do it!

A-1: Editing a Quick Mask

Here's how	Here's why
1 Open Puppy	In the current unit folder.
Save the image in Photoshop format as **My puppy**	You'll use the Magnetic Lasso tool to select the puppy, and then you'll clean up the selection by painting in Quick Mask mode.
2 Select the Magnetic Lasso tool	
3 Very quickly, draw a selection marquee around the puppy, as shown	(Click where you want to start the selection; then move the pointer around the dog *without* holding down the mouse button.) Don't add points to get an extremely accurate selection; you'll clean it up in Quick Mask mode.

4 In the toolbox, click as shown

(Click the Edit in Quick Mask Mode button to enter Quick Mask mode.)

The unselected areas of the image appear as transparent red. The red color is difficult to see against the brown background, so you'll change the mask color to blue.

5 Double-click

To open the Quick Mask Options dialog box.

Click the color swatch

To open the Select Quick Mask color dialog box.

In the R box, enter **0**

In the B box, enter **255**

Click **OK** twice

To return to the image.

6 Click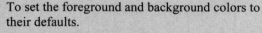

(If necessary.) To return to Quick Mask mode.

The blue color makes it easier to see the masked areas of the image. You'll now paint in Quick Mask mode to fine-tune the selection of the puppy.

7 Press ⒟

To set the foreground and background colors to their defaults.

Select the Brush tool

From the options bar, open the Brush Preset picker

Select the indicated brush

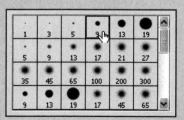

The 9-pixel hard brush.

Paint any areas that should be masked

(That is, paint those areas around the puppy that should *not* be part of the selection.) Painting with black adds to the masked area.

8 Press (X)   To switch the foreground and background colors. The foreground color is now white. Painting with white subtracts from the masked area.

Paint the areas of the dog that should be visible but are masked with blue

9 As necessary, press (X) to switch the foreground and background colors as you touch up the mask   Zoom in as necessary.

10 Update the image

Alpha channel masks

Explanation Another way that you can paint a masked area to add to or subtract from a selection is to paint in an *alpha channel* (an additional channel that doesn't contribute to the image itself, as color channels do). When you save a selection as an alpha channel, the alpha channel is created as an area of black and white pixels, with black representing masked areas, and white representing selected areas. In addition, gray areas in an alpha channel represent semi-selected areas, such as a feathered area.

To paint in an alpha channel to modify a saved selection:

1 In the Channels palette, click the alpha channel to display it in the image window. You can view the channel as a Quick Mask overlay over the image by showing the composite channel at the top of the Channels palette.

2 Paint with black to add to the masked area, and paint with white to add to the selected area.

3 Click the channel at the top of the Channels palette to view the image in the image window.

Do it!

A-2: Editing an alpha channel as a Quick Mask

Here's how	Here's why
1 In the toolbox, click as shown	
	(The Edit in Standard Mode button.) To view the selection as a marquee. Note that the selection is much more accurate than the original selection, which was created with the Magnetic Lasso tool.
2 Activate the Channels palette	
In the Channels palette, click	(The "Save selection as channel" button.) To save the selection in an alpha channel, which is named Alpha 1 by default.
3 Deselect the selection	Press Ctrl+D.
In the Channels palette, click **Alpha 1**	To display the channel in the image window. The selected areas of the image are white, and the unselected areas are black.
4 In the Channels palette, click the visibility column to the left of the RGB composite channel	To display the Alpha 1 channel as a Quick Mask overlay.

5 To the left of the dog, paint with white

To add to the selected area.

In the Channels palette, click the visibility column to the left of the RGB composite channel

To hide all channels except the Alpha 1 channel.

Observe the Alpha 1 channel in the image window

The area you painted is added to the mask.

6 In the Channels palette, click the **RGB** composite channel

(Click the channel itself, not the visibility column.) To show the image in the image window.

7 Choose **Select**, **Load Selection...**

To open the Load Selection dialog box.

Click **OK**

To load the Alpha 1 channel as a selection. The selected area now includes the area you just painted.

Deselect the selected area of the image

8 In the Channels palette, click the **Alpha 1** channel

To show the channel in the image window.

9 Paint with black on the white area you added next to the puppy

(Press X to switch the background and foreground colors.) To remove the extra area that you just painted.

10 In the Channels palette, click the **RGB** composite channel

To show the image in the image window.

11 Update the image

Topic B: Layer masks

This topic covers the following Adobe ACE exam objective for Photoshop CS3.

#	Objective
3.4	Explain how or why you would use a layer mask.

Creating layer masks

Explanation

When you want to show only part of a layer's contents, you can create a layer mask. That way, you can change which part of the layer is visible at any time, or you can reveal the entire layer again if necessary.

To create a layer mask, first select the part of the layer that you want to show. The unselected area of the layer will be hidden by the layer mask. Then, at the bottom of the Layers palette, click the Add layer mask button. The Layers palette will display a layer thumbnail and a layer mask thumbnail for that layer, as shown in Exhibit 2-2.

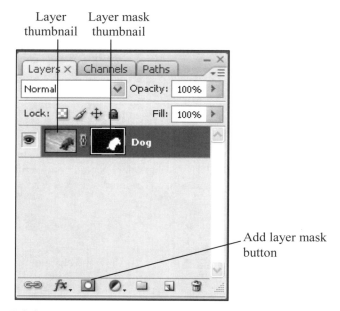

Exhibit 2-2: A layer containing a layer mask

Converting the Background layer

When you create a new Photoshop file with a white background, the image contains a single layer named Background. The Background layer is always the lowest layer in the stacking order. You cannot change the Background layer's blending mode or opacity, nor can you add a layer mask to it.

Because an image does not have to include a Background layer, you can convert it to a regular layer. To convert a Background layer to a regular layer:

1   In the Layers palette, double-click the Background layer to open the New Layer dialog box.

2   In the Name box, enter a name for the converted layer.

3   Click OK.

If you want to convert a regular layer to a Background layer, select it and choose Layer, New, Background from Layer. Each image can include only one Background layer. If you want to flatten all layers in an image down to a single Background layer, choose Layer, Flatten Image.

Do it!

B-1:   Creating a layer mask

Here's how	Here's why
1 Activate the Layers palette	You'll use a layer mask to isolate the dog from its background. You can't add a layer mask to the Background layer, though, so you'll convert it to a regular layer.
Double-click the Background layer	To open the New Layer dialog box.
In the Name box, enter **Dog**	
Click **OK**	To change the Background layer to a regular layer.
2 Activate the Channels palette	
Press [CTRL] and click the thumbnail for the Alpha 1 channel	To load the channel as a selection.
3 Activate the Layers palette	
Click 🔲	(The Add layer mask button.) To add a layer mask for the unselected area of the image. The dog is now visible over a transparent background.

4 Observe the Dog layer in the Layers palette

The Dog layer now has a layer thumbnail and a layer mask thumbnail.

Next, you'll add a solid white background to the image.

5 From the Swatches palette menu, choose **Small Thumbnail**

If necessary.

6 In the Layers palette, click [⊘.]

(The "Create new fill or adjustment layer" button.) To display a pop-up menu.

Choose **Solid Color...**

To create a solid-color fill layer. The "Pick a solid color" dialog box appears.

In the Swatches palette, click the white swatch

To specify a white color for the fill layer.

Click **OK**

To close the dialog box.

7 In the Layers palette, drag the new layer below the Dog layer

Now the dog appears over a white background.

8 Update the image

Editing layer masks

Explanation

After applying a layer mask to hide part of a layer, you might want to continue modifying the layer mask. To add to or subtract from a layer mask, you have to activate it by clicking the layer mask thumbnail. Otherwise, you'll be painting over the layer pixels themselves. When you activate the layer mask, the image's appearance in the image window doesn't change. However, when you paint with black in the image, you'll be adding to the mask (subtracting from the selection), and when you paint with white, you'll be adding to the selection.

If you want to return to editing the image itself, click the image thumbnail in the Layers palette. In addition, you can use the following techniques to change your view of the layer mask thumbnail:

- To view the layer mask in the image window, press Alt and click the layer mask thumbnail.
- To view the image in the image window, either click the layer thumbnail or press Alt and click the layer mask thumbnail.
- To disable the layer mask, revealing the entire layer, press Shift and click the layer mask thumbnail.
- To enable the layer mask, hiding the masked areas, press Shift and click the layer mask thumbnail.

Do it!

B-2: Editing a layer mask

Here's how	Here's why
1 Click the layer mask thumbnail in the Dog layer	(If necessary.) To activate the mask.
2 Paint with black on the areas outside the puppy that you want to add to the mask	To clean up the selection.
Press (X)	To switch the background and foreground colors.
Paint with white any areas of the puppy that you want to add to the selection	If necessary.
3 Choose **View**, **Fit on Screen**	If necessary.
4 Press (ALT) and click the layer mask thumbnail	To view the mask.
5 Click the layer thumbnail	To return to viewing the image.
6 Press (SHIFT) and click the layer mask thumbnail	
	To disable the layer mask. A red "X" appears over the layer mask thumbnail, and the entire layer is visible.
Press (SHIFT) and click the layer mask thumbnail	To re-enable the layer mask.
7 Update the image	

Topic C: Grayscale masks

This topic covers the following Adobe ACE exam objective for Photoshop CS3.

#	Objective
3.4	Explain how or why you would use a layer mask.

Softening mask edges

Explanation

You can paint with white and black in a mask to add to and subtract from a selection. However, you might want to create a layer mask that has soft or feathered edges. To specify a soft or feathered edge in a mask, apply a gray color. In a mask, shades of gray represent regions that are partially masked. Partially masked areas appear semi-transparent. The darker the gray color, the more transparent the layer contents will be through the mask.

To specify soft or feathered edges in a mask, you can use several techniques:

- Convert a feathered selection to a mask.
- Paint in the layer mask with a soft-edged brush.
- Apply a blur filter to the layer mask.

Do it! **C-1: Creating soft edges with a grayscale mask**

Here's how	Here's why
1 Fit the image on the screen	(If necessary.) For an advertisement, you'll create a soft-edged "thought bubble" containing a chicken dish.
2 Open Chicken	In the current unit folder.
Select the Move tool	
Drag the image from the Chicken window into the My puppy window	To create a new layer in the My puppy image.
Drag the chicken image so it snaps to the top-left corner of the My puppy image	
3 Name the new layer **Chicken dish**	
4 Select the Lasso tool	
On the options bar, set the Feather value to **10**	
Draw a cloud shape around the dish, as shown	

5 In the Layers palette, add a layer mask to the Chicken dish layer

(Click the Add layer mask icon.) To create a layer mask in the shape of the cloud. Because you specified a feather for the Lasso tool, the mask has soft edges.

Next, you'll add small clouds below the "thought bubble."

6 Select the Brush tool

   In the Brush Preset picker, select the indicated brush

The Soft Round 45 pixels brush.

   For the Chicken dish layer, verify that the layer mask thumbnail is selected

Not the layer thumbnail.

   Press X as necessary to set the foreground color to white

7 Between the dog and the cloud containing the chicken dish, paint two small cloud shapes, as shown

Painting in white on the layer mask removes the mask from the painted area, revealing the layer.

8 Zoom to 100% magnification

Observe that the edges of the puppy look too sharp against the white background. You'll use a filter to create a softer edge for the puppy.

9 Click the layer mask thumbnail for the Dog layer

You can apply filters to layer masks just as you'd apply them to image pixels.

Choose **Filter**, **Blur**, **Gaussian Blur...**

To open the Gaussian Blur dialog box.

In the Radius box, enter **2.0**

Click **OK**

To apply the blur to the layer mask. The dog's fur looks softer and more natural against the white background.

10 Choose **View**, **Fit on Screen**

11 Select the Chicken dish layer

Using the Move tool, drag the chicken dish around in the image

Both the layer mask and the underlying layer content move together because they're linked.

Click the chain icon between the layer thumbnail and the layer mask thumbnail, as shown

To unlink the layer from the layer mask.

Select the layer thumbnail

Using the Move tool, drag the chicken dish around in the image

The picture moves, while the thought balloon (created with the layer mask) stays in place.

12 Reposition the chicken dish as desired within the thought balloon

In the Chicken dish layer, click between the layer thumbnail and the layer mask thumbnail, as shown

To re-link the layer with the layer mask.

Next, you'll apply a drop shadow to the Dog layer to help make the puppy look more natural.

13 Select the Dog layer

    Click ☐ *fx.*   (The "Add a layer style" button.) To display the
                      Layer Style list.

    Select **Drop Shadow...**   To open the Layer Style dialog box. The Drop
                                  Shadow settings are already selected.

    In the Angle box, enter **90**

    In the Distance box, enter **6**

    In the Size box, enter **10**

    Click **OK**

To apply the drop shadow. The shadow appears
around the contours as defined by the layer
mask.

14 Update the image

    Close all open images

Gradient masks

Explanation

Another way to create a grayscale mask is to apply a gradient to part or all of a layer mask. Applying a gradient to a layer mask is useful when you want layer content to gradually fade across a specific area, rather than just display softened edges.

To apply a gradient to a layer mask:

1 Create a layer mask.
2 Select the Gradient tool.
3 In the Gradient Picker (opened from the options bar), select the Black, White gradient.
4 In the Layers palette, verify that the layer mask thumbnail is activated.
5 Drag across the image to specify the area you want to fade.

Do it!

C-2: Fading a layer with a gradient mask

Here's how	Here's why
1 Open Hawaii	In the current unit folder.
Save the image in Photoshop format as **My Hawaii**	You'll fade out the right side of the image to the white background, but you'll use a layer mask so you can change it later if you wish.
2 Select the Photo layer	If necessary.
3 Add a layer mask to the layer	(Click the Add layer mask button at the bottom of the Layers palette.) Because no part of the image was selected, the layer mask doesn't mask any of the image.
Verify that the layer mask thumbnail is selected	
4 Select the Gradient tool	
In the Gradient Picker, select the Black, White gradient, as shown	
Verify that the Linear Gradient option is selected	
	On the options bar.
Check **Reverse**	To reverse the gradient colors, so the gradient goes from white to black.

5 Show the document rulers

Choose View, Rulers.

Drag a horizontal gradient from the 2.75" mark on the horizontal ruler to the 3.75" mark

Because the gradient is drawn from white to black, the layer mask fades the layer out where the black becomes more predominant.

6 Update the image

Topic D: Clipping masks

This topic covers the following Adobe ACE exam objective for Photoshop CS3.

#	Objective
3.3	Explain how or why you would use a clipping group.

Creating clipping masks

Explanation

Another way to mask part of a layer is to create a *clipping mask*. When you create a clipping mask, you display the current layer over only the pixels in the layer below, as shown in Exhibit 2-3. The transparent space in the layer below specifies the areas that are masked in the layer above.

A clipping mask is unique because you're using the content of one layer to mask (hide) part of the content in another layer. Other types of masks are created as part of the layers they mask.

Clipping masks work well when you want to mask a layer based on content that might change. For example, you can clip (attach) a layer to a type layer below it so that the first layer's contents are visible only over the text on the type layer. Because a clipping mask is dynamic, you can change the text in the layer below, and the effect is automatically updated.

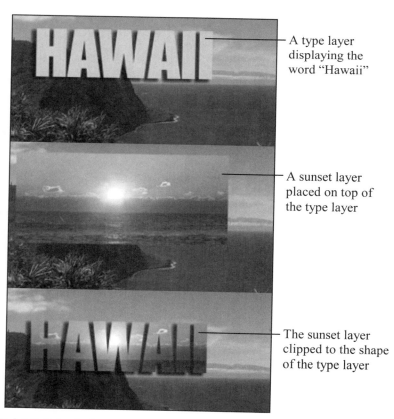

A type layer displaying the word "Hawaii"

A sunset layer placed on top of the type layer

The sunset layer clipped to the shape of the type layer

Exhibit 2-3: A clipping mask used with a type layer

A clipping mask can contain more than two layers. All of the layers clip to the shape of the bottommost layer.

To create a clipping mask:

1   Move the layer that you want to create a clipping mask for, so that it's directly above the layer whose content you want it to clip to.

2   To clip the layer to the layer below, do any of the following:

- Choose Layer, Create Clipping Mask.
- From the Layers palette menu, choose Create Clipping Mask.
- Press Alt, point to the line between the two layers in the Layers palette, and click.

You can move the layers independently of one another. If you want them to move together, you can link them by selecting them both and clicking the Link layers button in the Layers palette.

If you want to remove a clipping mask, you can use any of these techniques:

- Choose Layer, Release Clipping Mask.
- From the Layers palette menu, select Release Clipping Mask.
- Press Alt, point to the line between the two layers in the Layers palette, and click.

D-1: Clipping a layer to an underlying layer

Here's how	Here's why
1 Open Sunset	In the current unit folder.
2 Using the Move tool, drag the sunset image into the My Hawaii image	To create a new layer.
Name the new layer **Sunset**	
3 Drag to position the sun in the center of the "W" in "HAWAII"	When it's in the right position, the sun will be hidden behind the letter "W."
4 In the Layers palette, drag the Sunset layer above the HAWAII layer	You'll now clip the Sunset layer to the type layer below it.
5 From the Layers palette menu, choose **Create Clipping Mask**	 To create a clipping mask from the HAWAII layer.
6 Use the Move tool to drag the Sunset layer's contents	(If necessary.) To align the sun with the center of the "W."
7 Press (SHIFT) and click the HAWAII layer	(In the Layers palette.) To select the Sunset and HAWAII layers so you can link them.
Click	(The Link layers button.) To link the two layers. Any time you move the content of either of these layers, the content of both layers will move together.
8 In the image, drag the word "HAWAII"	To observe that the two layers move together.
9 Update My Hawaii	
Close all images	Don't save changes in the Sunset image.

Unit summary: Masks

Topic A   In this topic, you painted in **Quick Mask mode** to add to and subtract from a selection. In addition, you painted in an **alpha channel** to modify a selection.

Topic B   In this topic, you created a **layer mask** to hide part of a layer. In addition, you modified a layer mask.

Topic C   In this topic, you learned how to create **grayscale masks** to partially mask part of an image.

Topic D   In this topic, you applied a **clipping mask** to mask one layer based on the contents of the layer below.

Independent practice activity

In this activity, you'll use Quick Mask mode to edit a selection. You'll also create a layer mask and a clipping group. Finally, you'll apply a gradient layer mask.

1 Open Bowl of chiles practice. Save the image in Photoshop format as **My bowl of chiles practice**.

2 Select the Magic Wand tool. Set the Tolerance to **32** and check **Contiguous**, if necessary. Click the white space surrounding the chiles. Press Shift and click the white space not selected in one or two places to get most of the surrounding area selected.

3 Invert the selection so the chiles are selected. (*Hint*: Choose Select, Inverse.)

4 Edit the selection by painting in Quick Mask mode to improve the mask's accuracy.

   To do this step, click the Edit in Quick Mask Mode button in the toolbox. Press D to set the default background and foreground colors. Paint in black to add to the mask. Paint in white to add to the selection. Change brush sizes as needed.

5 Double-click the Background layer and rename it as **Bowl of chiles** to convert it to a regular layer.

6 Display the image in Standard mode, and convert the selection to a layer mask.

7 Open Turn up the heat practice, and save it in Photoshop format as **My turn up the heat practice**.

8 Drag the Bowl of chiles image into the "My turn up the heat practice" image. (*Hint*: Select the Move tool. The layer mask will be copied along with the layer).

9 In the Layers palette, drag the Bowl of chiles layer to the top of the layers, if necessary.

10 In the "My turn up the heat practice" image, adjust the Bowl of chiles layer mask by applying a Gaussian Blur with a Radius value of 1 pixel. (*Hint*: Be sure to click the layer mask thumbnail before applying the Gaussian Blur.)

11 Create a clipping group with the Flames and HEAT layers so that the flames appear only within the outlines of the letters. Adjust the position of the flames within the letters. (*Hint*: Because the layer that defines the shape must be on the bottom, move the Flames layer so it's above the HEAT layer, and choose Create Clipping Mask from the Layers palette menu. Then adjust the position of the flames.)

12 Fade out the black part of the Outlander logo on the right with a gradient layer mask, as shown in Exhibit 2-4.

To do this step, select the Outlander Logo layer and add a layer mask. With the layer mask thumbnail selected, select the Gradient tool. Verify that the Black, White gradient is selected and that Reverse is checked. Draw a gradient from the 2.5" mark on the horizontal ruler to the end of the logo.

13 Update and close all images.

Exhibit 2-4: The "My turn up the heat practice" image as it appears at the end of the independent practice activity

Review questions

1 How can you view a selection as a temporary colored overlay instead of as a marquee?

   A In the toolbox, click the Edit in Quick Mask Mode button.

   B Choose View, Extras.

   C Choose View, Show, Selection Edges to uncheck it.

   D Choose View, Show, None.

2 In Quick Mask mode, how can you add to a selection?

   A Choose Select, Modify, Expand.

   B Choose Select, Grow.

   C Paint using white.

   D Paint using black.

3 How can you use the Channels palette to add to a saved selection?

   A While viewing the image, Ctrl+click the alpha channel containing the selection; then paint with white.

   B While viewing the image, Ctrl+click the alpha channel containing the selection; then paint with black.

   C Click the alpha channel containing the selection to display it in the image window, and then paint with black.

   D Click the alpha channel containing the selection to display it in the image window, and then paint with white.

4 To view an alpha channel's contents as a colored overlay over the original image, you should:

   A Alt+click it.

   B Select it and enter Quick Mask mode.

   C Select it and view the composite RGB channels at the same time.

   D Choose View, Extras.

5 True or false: By default, the white part of a layer mask represents pixels that will be hidden.

6 True or false: The Background layer can contain a layer mask.

7 Which key do you press while clicking a layer mask thumbnail in the Layers palette to view the mask in the image window?

  A Alt

  B Ctrl

  C Shift

  D Caps Lock

8 Gray pixels in a layer mask make the corresponding image pixels:

  A More gray

  B Semi-transparent

  C Hard-edged

  D Inverted

9 Name two ways to create gray pixels within a layer mask.

10 Which layer in a clipping mask defines the shape to which the others are clipped?

  A The top layer in the clipping mask

  B The bottom layer in the clipping mask

  C The one you select when you apply the clipping mask

  D The one you hide by clicking in the Visibility column

11 Which methods can you use to create a clipping mask? [Choose all that apply.]

  A Press Alt, point to the line between two layers in the Layers palette, and click.

  B Create the bottom layer and choose Layer, Clip Layer Above to This One.

  C Select the layer that you want to clip to the layer below and choose Layer, Create Clipping Mask.

  D Select two layers and choose Layer, Group Layers.

Unit 3

Vector paths

Unit time: 70 minutes

Complete this unit, and you'll know how to:

A Use the path tools and commands to create vector paths.

B Use the path tools and options to edit vector paths.

C Use paths to create vector masks and clipping paths.

D Use paths to create vector-based artwork.

Topic A: Creating vector paths

This topic covers the following Adobe ACE exam objectives for Photoshop CS3.

#	Objective
6.1	Create shape layers and paths by using the Pen and Shape tools.
6.2	Explain the advantages of using vector drawing tools versus using raster drawing tools.
6.4	Create and edit paths by using the Paths palette.

Uses for vector paths

Explanation

Most images you work with in Photoshop are probably made up entirely of pixels. However, you can also create *vector paths* to define lines and areas geometrically instead of as a grid of pixels.

You can add vector paths to your images for several purposes, including:

- Selecting and masking image areas that have clearly defined shapes, such as smoothly flowing curves.
- Creating geometric graphics that are easy to draw and modify.
- Adding clipping paths to define transparent areas in an image that you plan to place in another application for print use.
- Flowing text or brush shapes along a path.

Using vector paths as selection masks and layer masks

When you want to select or mask part of an image that has a geometric shape, you'll often be able to create the selection or mask more quickly and accurately by using vector paths. In addition, vector paths don't increase the file size nearly as much as alpha channels do. After creating a path in the shape of the area you want to select or mask, you can convert the vector path to a selection or layer mask.

You can't directly use a vector path to partially mask image pixels, as you can by painting with gray in an alpha channel, in a pixel-based layer mask, or in Quick Mask mode. A vector path specifies which areas will be fully selected or masked and which areas will be fully outside the selection or mask. You can load a vector path as a selection, however, and then choose Select, Feather to specify a feathered selection.

Drawing geometric graphics

You can also use vector paths to draw geometric graphics in an image. You can use Photoshop's shape tools or pen tools to draw a shape so that a new shape layer is created automatically.

The shape layer is filled with the current fill color, but the shape you draw masks the color so that it appears only within the shape you drew. You can use the shape and pen tools to create geometric graphics that are much easier to modify and reshape than are pixel-based areas. When you flatten an image containing shape layers, the image's appearance doesn't change, but the vector paths themselves are removed, leaving only pixels.

Flowing text or brush shapes along a path

You can also use vector paths as guides along which text flows. For example, you can create a curving path, and add text whose baseline flows along that path. In addition, you can apply a stroke to the path based on a brush shape. The path then looks like it was drawn with the Brush tool.

Creating clipping paths

You might use Photoshop to create an image for use in another program, such as QuarkXPress. When you place a Photoshop image in a document designed for print output, not all programs will support transparency in the image.

For example, if you place a Photoshop image into a QuarkXPress file, any transparent areas in the image will appear with a solid fill. To ensure that an image retains its transparency when exported to a print application, you can use a vector path as a clipping path that specifies which area should be visible, leaving the area outside the clipping path transparent.

Vector tools

You can create and modify vector paths by using Photoshop's vector tools. The vector tools are stored in three tool groups in the toolbox:

- The *pen tools* and *path editing tools* are stored in the group that shows the Pen tool by default, as shown in Exhibit 3-1.

- The *shape tools* are stored in the group that shows the Rectangle tool by default, as shown in Exhibit 3-2.

- The *selection tools* are stored in the group that shows the Path Selection tool by default, as shown in Exhibit 3-3.

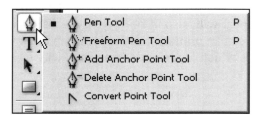

Exhibit 3-1: The pen and path editing tools

Exhibit 3-2: The shape tools

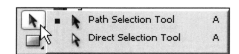

Exhibit 3-3: The selection tools

Path components

Paths created in Photoshop are made up of anchor points, segments, and direction points, as shown in Exhibit 3-4. The *anchor points* determine where the path flows. A *segment* is the part of a path between two anchor points. *Direction points* determine the curvature (if any) of each segment.

Direction points extend from anchor points. Each anchor point can have two direction points, with each one controlling the curvature of the segment on either side of the anchor point. If a segment contains no curvature, its anchor points won't have associated direction points.

Anchor point

Direction point

Segment

Exhibit 3-4: The components of a vector path

Do it!

A-1: Discussing the uses of vector paths

Question	Answer
1 In what circumstances might you want to use vector paths to specify an image selection?	
2 What is a benefit of drawing with the pen and shape tools instead of painting with the Brush or Pencil tools?	
3 What is the purpose of using a vector path as a clipping path?	

The Freeform Pen tool

You can use the Freeform Pen tool to draw paths of any shape, much as you can use the Lasso tool to create selections of any shape. When you select the Freeform Pen tool, the options bar displays the options shown in Exhibit 3-5.

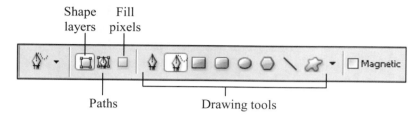

Exhibit 3-5: Some of the Freeform Pen tool options on the options bar

Several of the Freeform Pen tool options are described in the following table.

Item	Description
Shape layers icon	The paths you create generate *shape layers*. You can use a shape layer to add shapes filled with the current foreground color, or filled with a style that applies a gradient or pattern.
Paths icon	The paths you create generate *work paths*. You can use work paths to create vector paths that make no visible change in the image but can be used to create selections or clipping paths.
Fill pixels icon	The shapes you draw are painted directly on the current layer as pixels, rather than as vector paths. You can't modify these shapes by using the vector editing tools, but you can modify them as you'd modify any other raster data. This option is available with the shape tools, but not with the pen tools.
Drawing tool icons	Click a drawing tool icon to select that tool.
Magnetic check box	Check the Magnetic check box to convert the Freeform Pen tool to the Magnetic Pen tool so that the path you create will automatically snap to the image based on settings you specify. The Magnetic Pen tool operates similarly to the Magnetic Lasso tool.

To use the Magnetic Pen tool to draw a freeform vector path:

1 Select the Freeform Pen tool.

2 On the options bar, check Magnetic.

3 Point to where you want to begin the path, and click to add the first *fastening point*, which indicates where the path begins.

4 Move the pointer within the image to specify the shape of the path. As you move the pointer, fastening points appear along the path to specify where the path flows. You can click to add a fastening point where you want one, and you can press Backspace or Delete to remove the last fastening point added.

5 Point to the first fastening point (where you started the path), and when the pointer displays a small circle, click to close the path. You can also double-click at any time to complete the path with a segment connecting the last fastening point to the first one.

Saving paths

When you create a path with the Paths option selected on the options bar, the new path is added as a work path, as shown in Exhibit 3-6. The work path is visible in the image, and it appears in the Paths palette with the name "Work Path."

The work path you've created is temporary. If you click a blank part of the Paths palette to deselect the work path, and then draw a new path, the new one will replace the old one. You can save a work path, however, as a path that won't be removed until you delete it.

To save a work path as a permanent path:

1   In the Paths palette, double-click Work Path to open the Save Path dialog box.

2   In the Name box, enter a name for the path.

3   Click OK.

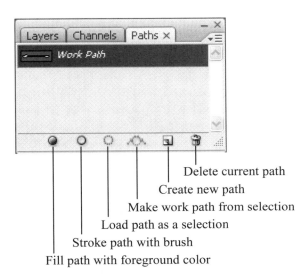

Delete current path
Create new path
Make work path from selection
Load path as a selection
Stroke path with brush
Fill path with foreground color

Exhibit 3-6: The Paths palette

Selecting paths and path components

The technique you use to select a path depends on what you want to do with the path:

- To show the path in the image window, you can click a path in the Paths palette. You can then create a selection from the path, apply or adjust a fill or stroke, and more. To hide any paths in the image, you can click a blank area of the Paths palette.

- To display the path's anchor points, you can click a path with the Path Selection tool. You can then drag the path to move it.

- To display the associated direction points, you can click a segment or anchor point with the Direct Selection tool. You can then drag direction points and anchor points to reshape the path.

Do it! **A-2: Creating a freeform path**

Here's how	Here's why
1 Open Measuring spoon	In the current unit folder.
Save the image in Photoshop format as **My measuring spoon**	You'll use the Freeform Pen tool to draw a path that traces the outline of the spoon.
2 In the toolbox, click and hold [pen icon]	To display the pen tools.
Select the **Freeform Pen Tool**	
On the options bar, click [icon]	(The Paths icon.) To specify that the paths you draw will generate work paths, rather than shape layers.
On the options bar, check **Magnetic**	To convert the Freeform Pen tool to the Magnetic Pen tool.
3 Click an edge of the spoon	To place the first fastening point, which determines where the path begins.
Move the pointer around the spoon	Additional fastening points appear along the path as you move the pointer.
When the pointer is over the initial fastening point, click the mouse	(Point to the initial fastening point, and when the pointer displays a small circle, click.) To close the path.
4 Activate the Paths palette	An entry named Work Path appears, representing the path you just created. You'll save the work path.

5 In the Paths palette, double-click **Work Path**

   In the Name box, enter **Spoon freeform**

   Click **OK**

To open the Save Path dialog box.

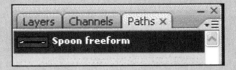

To save the path.

6 Zoom in on the image

To observe the inaccuracies in the path.

7 In the toolbox, click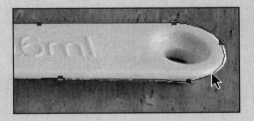

(The Path Selection tool.) You can use the Path Selection tool to select and manipulate a path.

   Click the edge of the path as shown

To select the path so that its anchor points are visible.

8 Click in the image window, away from the path

To deselect the path anchor points.

9 Click the blank area of the Paths palette

To deselect the path. The path is no longer visible in the image window.

10 Update the file

Converting selections to paths

Explanation

Another way to create a path is to convert a selection to a path. This is particularly useful when you want to generate a path for an item that you can select easily with the selection tools.

To convert a selection to a path, click the "Make work path from selection" icon in the Paths palette. The new path is created with the default settings. If you want to control how accurately the path matches the shape of the original selection, then, before you convert the selection to a path, change settings in the Make Work Path dialog box.

To open the Make Work Path dialog box, do either of the following:

- From the Paths palette menu, choose Make Work Path.
- Press Alt and click the "Make work path from selection" icon.

In the Make Work Path dialog box, you can specify a Tolerance value. The lower the tolerance, the more closely the path will match the shape of the original selection. In addition, a lower tolerance will generate a path with more anchor points. A higher tolerance will generate a smoother path with fewer anchor points, but the path won't conform as closely to the original shape of the selection.

Do it!

A-3: Converting a selection to a path

Here's how	Here's why
1 In the Layers palette, select the Spoon layer	If necessary.
2 Select the Magic Wand tool	
Set the Tolerance value to **60**	
Click the spoon, as shown	
3 Press (SHIFT) and click other areas on the measuring spoon to add to the selection	To select all areas of the spoon.
4 Select the Lasso tool	
Press (SHIFT) and drag around the spices in the spoon	
	(Drag around any other areas necessary.) To add them to the selection.

5 In the Paths palette, click [icon]	(The "Make work path from selection" icon.) To create a path from the selection you just made.
Double-click **Work Path**	To open the Save Path dialog box.
Name the path **Spoon selection** and click **OK**	To create the path.
6 In the toolbox, click [icon]	The Path Selection tool.
In the image window, click the path	To observe the number of points and the accuracy and smoothness of the path.
	You'll deselect the path and create a second, more accurate path.
Deselect the path	In the Paths palette, click a blank area below the path.
7 Choose **Select**, **Reselect**	To select the most recent selection.
From the Paths palette menu, choose **Make Work Path...**	To open the Make Work Path dialog box.
In the Tolerance box, enter **1**	
Click **OK**	To create the work path.
Name the work path **Spoon selection 1 pixel**	Double-click the new path in the Paths palette, type the new name, and click OK.
8 Using the Path Selection tool, select the path you just created	Observe that the path is more accurate, but contains more points.
Deselect the path	Click in a blank area of the Paths palette.
9 Update the image	

The Pen tool

Explanation

Another way to create a path is to use the Pen tool. When you use the Pen tool to create a path, you have more control over the path's shape than is possible to get with other methods. With the Pen tool, you specify the location of anchor points and direction points to create straight or curving segments with precision.

Straight segments

To create a straight segment, click to place two anchor points, as shown in Exhibit 3-7. A straight segment appears between the two anchor points, and there are no direction points. You can continue clicking to add more segments to the path.

To begin a new path, press Esc or click the Pen tool in the toolbox. A small "×" appears next to the Pen tool's pointer when it's ready to begin a new path. If you want to draw a horizontal, vertical, or 45-degree segment, press Shift as you click to add the second anchor point.

Exhibit 3-7: A straight segment connecting two anchor points

Curving segments

To create a curving segment, point to where you want to begin the path. Then click and drag in the direction you want the path to curve. Point to where you want to add the second anchor point, and drag in the direction you want the path to move as it enters the second anchor point.

For example, to create a rainbow shape, drag up to indicate that the path should curve upward from the first anchor point, as shown in Exhibit 3-8. Point to where you want to place the second anchor point, and drag down to indicate that the path should curve downward as it enters that anchor point, as shown in Exhibit 3-9.

Exhibit 3-8: The first anchor point and direction point for a curving segment

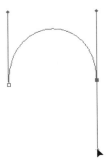

Exhibit 3-9: A curving segment

Smooth points and corner points

When you drag to create an anchor point with a direction point, a second direction point is created to control the curvature of the next segment. By default, the next segment will continue the first segment's curve direction. So if a segment curves downward into its second anchor point, the path will continue to curve downward as it leaves that anchor point for the next segment. When the segments on either side of an anchor point curve in the same direction, that anchor point is called a *smooth point*, shown in Exhibit 3-10.

Smooth point

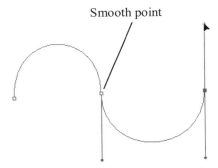

Exhibit 3-10: Two segments connected by a smooth point

You can specify a different direction for the second segment, thereby creating a *corner point*. To draw a path's second segment with a corner point, press Alt to temporarily select the Convert Point tool; then drag the existing direction point for the next segment to specify the direction you want the next segment to curve, as shown in Exhibit 3-11.

You can then release Alt to return to the Pen tool, and drag to specify the ending anchor point and direction point for the segment, as shown in Exhibit 3-12. Dragging a direction point by using the Convert Point tool converts a smooth point to a corner point. You can do this while drawing a path or after completing a path.

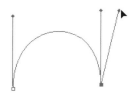

Exhibit 3-11: Dragging a direction point by using the Convert Point tool to specify a corner point

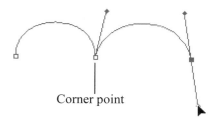

Corner point

Exhibit 3-12: Two segments connected by a corner point

If you click twice to create a straight segment, you can drag from the second anchor point to create a single direction point to specify the curvature for the next segment without affecting the existing straight segment.

In addition, if you want to draw a straight segment following a curving segment, you can press Alt and click the curving segment's second anchor point to remove the direction point that would have applied curvature to the following segment. The existing curving segment won't be affected.

Do it!   **A-4:   Creating paths with the Pen tool**

Here's how	Here's why
1 Choose **View**, **Fit on Screen**	If necessary.
In the toolbox, click and hold [pen icon]	The Freeform Pen tool.
Select the **Pen Tool**	You'll begin drawing a path around the spoon by creating a straight segment along the spoon's top edge.
2 Click as shown	
	To place the first anchor point of the straight segment. After you click to add the first point, the pointer's "×" symbol disappears to indicate that additional clicks will add to this path, rather than begin a new path.
3 Click as shown	
	To complete the initial straight segment.
4 From the anchor point you just created, drag left and slightly up, as shown	
	To create the initial point of a curved segment.

5 Click and hold as shown

Hold the mouse button down.

Drag down and slightly to the left, as shown

To create the curved segment around the top of the spoon's well.

6 Click and hold as shown

Hold the mouse button down.

Drag up and to right, as shown

To create the curved segment at the bottom of the spoon.

7 Press (ALT) and drag the top-right direction point you just created, as shown

To allow the right direction point to move at an independent angle, so you can create a sharp corner.

8 Click as shown

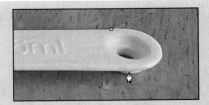

To create a straight segment at the bottom of the spoon.

9 From the anchor point you just created, drag right as shown

To begin a curved segment for the end of the spoon.

10 On the first anchor point you created, drag left as shown

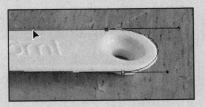

To complete the path.

11 In the Paths palette, save the work path as **Spoon pen**

12 Update the file

Topic B: Editing vector paths

This topic covers the following Adobe ACE exam objective for Photoshop CS3.

#	Objective
6.1	Create shape layers and paths by using the Pen and Shape tools.

Modifying paths

Explanation

After creating a path, you can change its shape. You can add and remove anchor points and direction points, convert smooth points to corner points, and drag segments, anchor points, and direction points.

The Direct Selection tool

To modify a path, you can use the Direct Selection tool and the following techniques:

- Drag a curving segment to increase or decrease its curvature without changing the angle of the direction points.
- Drag a direction point to adjust the curvature of its associated segment.
- Drag an anchor point to move it; this adjusts the segments on either side of the anchor point.

When you drag a direction point attached to a smooth point, the other direction point connected to the anchor point moves as well. To move a direction point independently, use the Convert Point tool to drag it. When you use the Convert Point tool to drag a direction point, you convert the smooth point to a corner point.

Do it!

B-1: Adjusting path points

Here's how	Here's why
1 Zoom in to 300% on the well of the spoon	
2 In the toolbox, click and hold [icon]	The Path Selection tool.
Select the **Direct Selection Tool**	You'll drag segments, anchor points, and direction points to adjust the path's shape.
Click the path	To select it and view the anchor points.
3 Drag the anchor points to just inside the edges of the spoon	If necessary.

4 At the top of the spoon, adjust the positions of the anchor and direction points, as shown

To make the path match the spoon fairly closely. You can press Alt and drag a direction point separately from its corresponding direction point.

At the left side of the spoon, adjust the positions of the anchor and direction points, as shown

At the bottom of the spoon, adjust the positions of the anchor and direction points, as shown

Adding and removing anchor points

Explanation

After completing a path, you can add or remove anchor points to continue adjusting the path's shape. To add a point, you can use either the Pen tool or the Add Anchor Point tool to point to any path segment and click. When you use the Pen tool to point to a path segment, the pointer displays a plus sign (+), indicating that clicking will add an anchor point.

You can remove an anchor point by using either the Pen tool or the Delete Anchor Point tool; just point to the anchor point and click. When you use the Pen tool to point to an anchor point, the mouse pointer displays a minus sign (-), indicating that clicking will delete the anchor point.

Do it!

B-2: Changing the number of anchor points

Here's how	Here's why
1 Scroll to the other end of the spoon	
2 Try to drag the rightmost path segment to match the spoon	The path can't match the shape closely with only the two points defining the curved segment.
3 Using the Pen tool, click as shown	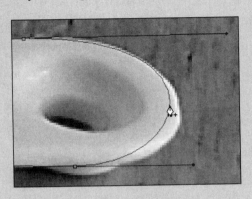 To add another anchor point to the curve.
4 Using the Direct Selection tool, drag to position the anchor point and its direction points in the positions and angles shown	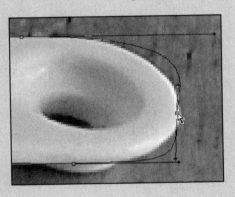 The anchor point controls the position of the path. The direction points control the severity and angle of the curve.
5 Drag the anchor points and direction points as necessary to closely match the spoon curvature	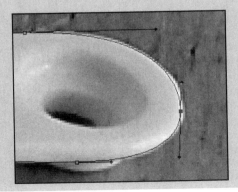

Subpaths

Explanation

When a path is selected in the Paths palette, any new paths you create are added as *subpaths*. Creating subpaths is useful when you want to use paths to generate a selection or create a mask made up of more than one area or shape. When you create subpaths, you can use buttons on the options bar, shown in Exhibit 3-13, to specify how the paths will interact with each other where they overlap.

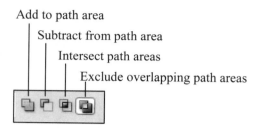

Exhibit 3-13: Buttons for combining subpaths

The buttons for combining subpaths are described in the following table.

Button	Description
Add to path area	The area within new subpaths you draw is added to the original path. A selection or mask generated from the paths includes the area within all the paths.
Subtract from path area	New subpaths you draw remove any part of the original path that they overlap. A selection or mask generated from the paths includes only the area of the original path that's not overlapped by any of the subpaths.
Intersect path areas	A new subpath you draw restricts the path to the area where it intersects with the original path. A selection or mask generated from the paths includes only the area where the two paths intersect.
Exclude overlapping path areas	A new subpath you draw is added to the path area, but overlapping areas are removed. A selection or mask generated from the paths includes the area within all paths, except for the areas where they overlap.

After creating a path, you can apply a different path area button to it. To do so, use the Path Selection tool to select the subpath, and click the path area button you want.

Converting paths to selections

You can convert a path in the Paths palette to a selection by using either of these techniques:

- Select the path in the Paths palette and click the "Load path as a selection" button.
- Press Ctrl and click the path in the Paths palette.

Do it!   **B-3:   Combining subpaths to form a single path**

Here's how	Here's why
1 Select the Pen tool	You'll create a small visible hole in the spoon because you want the background to show through it when you use the path as a mask.
2 In the Paths palette, verify that the Spoon pen path is selected	You'll add a subpath to it.
3 Create an anchor point and direction points, as shown	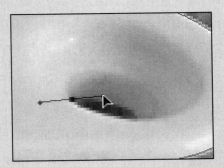
4 Create a second anchor point and direction points, as shown	
5 Press (ALT) and drag the second direction point of the anchor point you just created, as shown	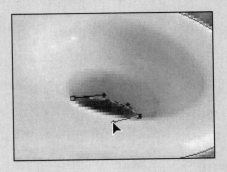 To make a sharp corner in the path.
Press (ALT) and drag the initial point of the path	 To create another sharp corner.

6 Verify that the "Exclude overlapping path areas" button is selected on the options bar

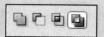

This option will cause the new subpath to cut a hole in the original path when you load it as a selection.

7 While pressing CTRL, click **Spoon pen** in the Paths palette

To load the path as a selection.

8 Choose **Select**, **Inverse**

To invert the selection.

Press ← BACKSPACE

To delete the background. The black layer created below the spoon shows through the hole.

Choose **Edit**, **Undo Clear**

To bring back the background.

Deselect the current selection

You'll now add another subpath to create the bump at the bottom of the spoon handle.

9 In the Paths palette, select **Spoon pen**

When a path is selected, any new path you create acts as a subpath.

In the toolbox, select the **Ellipse Tool**, as shown

Drag to create a path, as shown

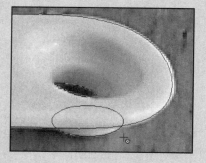

10 Select the Path Selection tool

11 Press CTRL and click **Spoon pen**

(In the Paths palette.) To convert the paths to a selection.

12 Invert the selection

    Press `← BACKSPACE`

To delete the background. The black layer below shows through the top half of the ellipse; this wasn't your intent.

    Press `CTRL` + `Z`

To restore the background.

    Deselect the current selection

You'll apply the "Add to path area" option to this subpath, rather than the "Exclude overlapping path areas" option.

13 Click **Spoon pen**

(In the Paths palette.) To select the path.

    Using the Path Selection tool, click the ellipse path

This path should add to, and not exclude, the original path when combined with the outer path.

    On the options bar, click

The "Add to shape area" button.

14 Press `CTRL` and click **Spoon pen**

(In the Paths palette.) To convert the path to a selection.

    Invert the selection

    Press `← BACKSPACE`

To delete the background. The elliptical subpath now adds to the shape area as intended.

    Press `CTRL` + `Z`

To restore the background

    Deselect the current selection

15 Update the file

Topic C: Vector masks

This topic covers the following Adobe ACE exam objective for Photoshop CS3.

#	Objective
6.4	Create and edit paths by using the Paths palette.

Creating vector masks

Explanation

In addition to using vector paths to create selections, you can use vector paths to create vector masks. You can also use vector paths to generate layer masks and clipping paths.

A *vector mask* works the same way as a layer mask. However, you might be able to create and modify a vector mask more easily and with greater precision. After creating a path, you can load it as a selection and create a standard layer mask from the selection.

When you generate a vector mask directly from a vector path, the mask's edges retain their crispness, and you'll be able to use the vector tools to easily modify the vector mask's shape. A single layer can include both a vector mask and a layer mask.

To create a vector mask from a path:

1   In the Paths palette, select the path that you want to use as a mask.
2   In the Layers palette, select the layer you want to mask.
3   Choose Layer, Vector Mask, Current Path.

Do it!

C-1:   Creating a vector mask

Here's how	Here's why
1 Undock the Paths palette from its current group	(Drag the Paths palette tab away from the group.) So you can see the Paths and Layers palettes at the same time.
2 In the Paths palette, select the Spoon pen path	
3 In the Layers palette, select the Spoon layer	If necessary.
4 Choose **Layer**, **Vector Mask**, **Current Path**	The black background from the layer below appears around the spoon. You can modify the vector mask at any time by using the path tools.
5 Update the image	

Clipping paths

Explanation

You might use images from Photoshop in documents designed for print use. If an image in Photoshop includes transparent areas, that transparency will still be in effect when you print the image from many other programs, including Adobe InDesign and Adobe Illustrator.

However, some programs, such as QuarkXPress, don't support Photoshop's transparency and will print transparent areas from the image as solid colored areas. In those cases, you can use Photoshop to specify a *clipping path*, which specifies that only areas within it are printed, leaving areas outside the clipping path transparent.

When you add a clipping path to an image in Photoshop, you have to save the image in Photoshop, EPS, or TIFF format, each of which supports clipping paths. You cannot use clipping paths to specify transparent areas for Web graphics. When you want to create Web images with transparent areas, you can use the GIF and PNG formats, which support transparency.

Flatness

When you designate a path as a clipping path, you can specify a *flatness* value for it. When you print to a device using the PostScript printing language, smooth vector curves are output as a series of tiny straight segments. The smaller the straight segments are, the more of them are needed to reproduce the curve, resulting in a smoother curve. However, the smaller the straight segments are, the more memory is required during printing. You can specify a higher flatness value to indicate that curves should be rendered using fewer straight segments, thereby requiring less memory during printing.

When you print a file containing an image with a clipping path, you might get an error message if the flatness value is too low. If that happens, you should enter a higher flatness value. If you're printing to a low-resolution printer, use a flatness value of about 3. For high-resolution printers, use a flatness value of up to 10. You might also need to increase the flatness value if the clipping path includes too many anchor points.

Specifying a clipping path

To create a clipping path:

1   From the Paths palette menu, choose Clipping Path to open the Clipping Path dialog box.
2   From the Path list, select the path you want to convert to a clipping path.
3   In the Flatness box, enter a flatness value.
4   Click OK.

Do it!

C-2: Creating a clipping path

Here's how	Here's why
1 From the Paths palette menu, choose **Clipping Path...**	To open the Clipping Path dialog box.
2 From the Path list, select **Spoon pen**	
3 In the Flatness box, enter **10**	A flatness value of 10 is appropriate for a high-resolution printer.
Click **OK**	To create the clipping path.
4 Update the image	

Topic D: Paths for creative imagery

This topic covers the following Adobe ACE exam objectives for Photoshop CS3.

#	Objective
6.1	Create shape layers and paths by using the Pen and Shape tools.
6.3	Given a scenario, alter the properties of type.

Paths as graphics

Explanation

In addition to creating paths as clipping paths, as masks, or for generating selections, you can create paths as actual graphics that appear in your image. For example, you can adjust the shape of text characters, create a path on which to flow text, apply a brush stroke to a path, or create vector shapes that display a fill.

Converting type to paths

The font files you use to create type define each character as a vector path. Ordinarily, you don't see or adjust the points and path segments, but they're used to generate the shapes with smooth edges at any size. Photoshop allows you to convert text layers back to the original vector paths, which you can then adjust to change the character shapes, as shown in Exhibit 3-14.

To convert type to a path:

1   Select the type layer.
2   Either right-click the type layer or choose Layer, Type. Then choose a command to convert the type:

- If you want to replace the type layer with a shape layer that looks identical (but has editable path shapes), choose Convert to Shape.

- If you want the type layer to remain, and you want to add the path outlines to the Paths palette as the work path, choose Create Work Path.

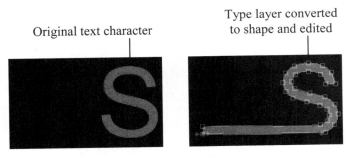

Exhibit 3-14: Type converted to a shape

Do it!

D-1: Converting type characters to editable shapes

Here's how	Here's why
1 Open Outlander logo rework	
Save the file in Photoshop format as **My Outlander logo rework**	You'll extend the bottom-left side of the "S" in "Spices" to the guide that aligns with the "O" in "Outlander." You'll duplicate the Spices layer first to retain the original version.
2 Display the View menu and verify that Extras is checked	In this image, when you check Extras, a vertical guide appears, extending down along the left edge of the "O" in "Outlander."
3 Drag the Spices layer to the "Create a new layer" icon	To create a Spices copy layer.
Hide the Spices layer	
4 Right-click the **Spices copy** layer	
Choose **Convert to Shape**	To convert the type to a shape layer with a vector mask in the shape of the text characters.
5 Select the Direct Selection tool	To begin editing the path.
6 Click the **S** at the beginning of "Spices"	
	You'll delete some anchor points at the bottom-left side in order to extend the bottom of the character to the left.
7 Drag a marquee to select the six anchor points as shown, and stop to the left of the bottommost anchor point	
8 Press DELETE	

9 Drag a selection marquee around the bottom two anchor points, as shown

10 Drag the bottommost anchor point to the guide, as shown

11 In the Layers palette, click below the Black layer

Observe the text

To deselect the Spices copy layer and hide its path outlines.

12 Update and close
My Outlander logo rework

Type on a path

To add text that flows along a path:

1　In the toolbox, select a Type tool.

2　In the Paths palette, select the path whose shape you want the text to flow along.

3　In the image window, click the path at the location where you want to begin adding text. A flashing insertion point appears. A new type layer appears in the Layers palette, and a new type path appears in the Paths palette, containing a copy of the original path you clicked.

4　Specify the text formatting you want on the options bar, and type to add the text that will flow along the path.

You can also click within a closed path to add type that flows within the path.

Do it!

D-2:   Wrapping type on a path

Here's how	Here's why
1 Select the Spoon pen path	If necessary.
Choose **View**, **Fit on Screen**	
2 Press D	To select the default colors.
Press X	To exchange colors, so the foreground color is white and the background color is black.
3 Using the Horizontal Type tool, click the leftmost part of the path, as shown	
On the options bar, set the type to **Arial**, **12 pt**	
4 Type **Just a little goes a looooong way...**	
5 Select **looooong** and the spaces before and after it	
6 On the options bar, click	(The "Toggle the Character and Paragraph palettes" button.) To open the Character palette.
In the Character palette, point to AV and drag to the right	
	To scrub the tracking value, spreading the word "looooong" out significantly.
Close the Character and Paragraph palettes	Click the "Toggle the Character and Paragraph palettes" button.
On the options bar, click ✔	To complete the edit.
7 Select the Move tool	
Press SHIFT + ↑ twice	
	To move the text up 20 pixels.
8 Update the image	

Shape layers

Explanation

You can also use vector paths to draw geometric graphics in an image. You can use Photoshop's shape tools or pen tools to draw a shape, so that a new shape layer is created automatically. A *shape layer* is actually a solid fill layer with a vector mask. Creating shapes by using a shape layer is useful when you want to be able to easily edit and scale the shape with path editing tools.

To draw filled shapes by using the shape tools:

1 In the toolbox or on the options bar, select a shape tool.

2 On the options bar, click the Shape Layers button.

3 On the options bar, use the Style list to specify a fill style for the shape, if you want to use one.

4 In the image, drag to create the shape.

5 Double-click the new shape layer to open the Layer Style dialog box. Apply custom styles to the shape and click OK.

Do it!

D-3: Creating a vector shape layer

Here's how	Here's why
1 In the Layers palette, select the Spoon layer	
2 Select the Rounded Rectangle tool	
On the options bar, set the Radius value to **10 pixels**	If necessary.
On the options bar, click [icon]	The Shape Layers button.
3 Create a rounded rectangle, as shown	loooong way...
4 Double-click the Shape 1 layer	To open the Layer Style dialog box.
Under Styles, click **Bevel and Emboss**	To display the Bevel and Emboss settings.
Under Structure, in the Size box, enter **10**	
Under Styles, click **Gradient Overlay**	To display the Gradient Overlay settings.
From the Gradient list, select **Orange, Yellow, Orange**	

5 Click **OK**

To close the Layer Style dialog box.

6 In the Paths palette, click a blank area below the named paths

To deselect the paths. You'll add type on top of the new button shape, and you'll need to position the type separately from the shape.

7 Press (X)

To set the foreground color to black.

8 Select the Horizontal Type tool

Reset the Tracking value to **0**

(In the Character palette.) If necessary.

Click near the left side of the button

Type **Click for info**

9 Use the Move tool to position the text over the shape

If necessary.

10 Update the image

Stroking paths

Explanation

Another way to use a path as an artistic element in an image is to create a brush stroke based on the path's shape. When you create a brush stroke based on a path, the stroke follows the shape of all paths and subpaths, regardless of the options you specified for how the subpaths interact.

If a path includes overlapping subpaths, and you want to apply a brush stroke to only the outer border of the overlapping paths, then you should first combine the overlapping subpaths into a single path.

To apply a brush stroke to a path:

1 In the Paths palette, select the path you want to stroke. If the path includes overlapping subpaths that you want to combine, then follow these steps:

    a If you want to keep a copy of the original path with the subpaths, then drag the path to the Create new path button in the Paths palette to make a copy.

    b In the duplicate path, use the Path Selection tool to select each subpath you want to combine.

    c On the options bar, click Combine.

2 In the Layers palette, select the layer that you want the stroke to appear on.

3 In the toolbox, select the Brush tool.

4 In the Brush Preset picker, select the brush you want to use.

5 In the Paths palette, click the "Stroke path with brush" button.

Do it!

D-4: Stroking a path with a brush shape

Here's how	Here's why
1 Hide the Spoon layer	You'll experiment with making a creative stroked outline of the measuring spoon instead of a photograph.
2 Above the Spoon layer, create a layer named **Drawn spoon**	
3 Set the foreground color to white	Press X.
4 Select the Brush tool	
Select the 33-pixel **Hard Pastel on Canvas** brush, as shown	From the Brush Preset picker.
5 Select the Spoon pen path	

6 In the Paths palette, click 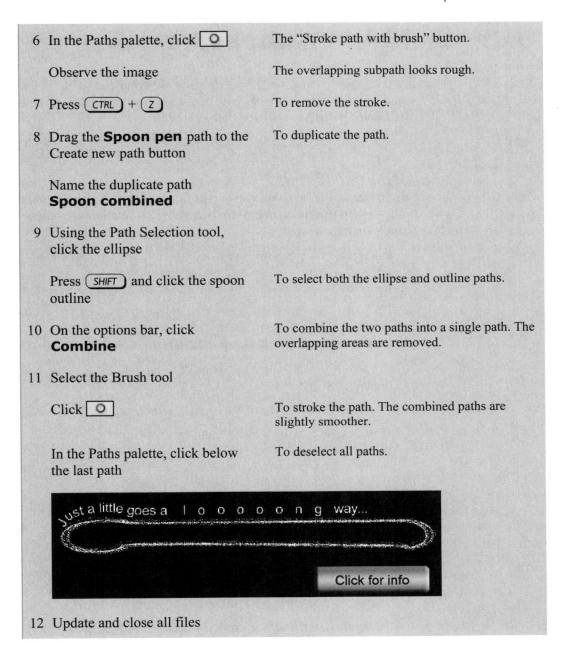 The "Stroke path with brush" button.

Observe the image The overlapping subpath looks rough.

7 Press (CTRL) + (Z) To remove the stroke.

8 Drag the **Spoon pen** path to the Create new path button To duplicate the path.

Name the duplicate path **Spoon combined**

9 Using the Path Selection tool, click the ellipse

Press (SHIFT) and click the spoon outline To select both the ellipse and outline paths.

10 On the options bar, click **Combine** To combine the two paths into a single path. The overlapping areas are removed.

11 Select the Brush tool

Click To stroke the path. The combined paths are slightly smoother.

In the Paths palette, click below the last path To deselect all paths.

12 Update and close all files

Unit summary: Vector paths

Topic A In this topic, you learned about the uses of **vector paths** in Photoshop. You also learned how to use the **pen tools** to draw paths, and you converted selections to paths. Finally, you saved paths by using the Paths palette.

Topic B In this topic, you used the Direct Selection tool to reshape paths by adjusting **anchor points**, **direction points**, and **segments**. You also added and removed anchor points, and you created **subpaths**.

Topic C In this topic, you used **vector masks** to mask layer content. You also designated a path as a **clipping path** to specify transparent areas of an image when printed from a desktop publishing application.

Topic D In this topic, you converted **type** to paths and wrapped type along a path. In addition, you used the shape tools to add **vector-based shapes** to an image, and you applied layer styles to the shapes. Finally, you created brush strokes that flowed along the shape of a path.

Independent practice activity

In this activity, you'll create a path and a subpath. In addition, you'll use a path to create a clipping path and a vector mask.

1 Open Spice bottle. Save the image in Photoshop format as **My spice bottle**.

2 Create a path extending from the top-left corner of the bottle, down around the bottle bottom, and up to the top-right corner, as shown in Exhibit 3-15. Don't include the top curve. (*Hint*: Use the Pen tool, and on the options bar, click the Paths button. Make anchor points as needed.)

3 Using the Ellipse tool, make a subpath for the top of the bottle, as shown in Exhibit 3-16. (*Hint*: Specify the "Add to path area" option for the ellipse.)

4 Save the work path as a path named **Bottle**.

5 Specify that the path act as a clipping path, to specify transparency outside the bottle when you place the image in a file for print use. (*Hint*: From the Paths palette menu, choose Clipping Path. Enter a flatness value of 10.)

6 Make this path a vector mask for the Bottle layer, as shown in Exhibit 3-17. (*Hint*: Be sure the Bottle layer is selected in the Layers palette, and the Bottle path is selected in the Paths palette. Then, choose the command.)

7 Update and close all files.

Exhibit 3-15: The path as it appears after Step 2 of the independent practice activity

Exhibit 3-16: The path as it appears after Step 3

Exhibit 3-17: The path as it appears after Step 6

Review questions

1 Which tool cannot directly create a vector path?

  A Pen

  B Rectangle

  C Custom Shape

  D Lasso

2 How can you create a shape layer that displays an oval filled with a solid color?

  A Select the Elliptical Marquee tool and drag in the image.

  B Select the Ellipse tool and drag in the image.

  C Select the Lasso tool and drag in the image.

  D Create a new layer; then select the Elliptical Marquee tool and drag in the image.

3 True or false: A vector path must pass through each direction point.

4 To choose exactly where anchor and direction points will be placed along a vector path as you create it, which tool should you use?

A Ellipse

B Lasso

C Polygon

D Pen

5 Which of the following are advantages of using vector drawing tools versus using raster drawing tools? [Choose all that apply.]

A Adding or removing selected areas in Quick Mask mode.

B Selecting and masking image areas that have clearly defined shapes, such as smoothly flowing curves.

C Creating paths in the Paths palette that store semi-transparency information.

D Creating geometric graphics that are easy to draw and modify.

6 You want to create a solid-colored geometric object whose shape you can easily modify later. Which type of tools should you use to create the shape?

A Vector drawing tools

B Selection tools

C Raster drawing tools

D Pixel-based drawing tools

7 A path's _____ points determine the curvature of its segments.

8 True or false: A path that appears in the Paths palette might contain a secondary path called a subpath.

9 To hide parts of a layer with a vector path, as you would with a layer mask, what should you create?

10 True or false: "Vector mask" and "clipping path" are interchangeable terms.

11 Name three ways to use vector paths that appear directly in the image, not just in the Paths palette.

12 You want to flow type along a curving path. What should you do?

   A Use a Path Type tool.

   B Select the path in the Paths palette, and click with a Type tool at the location where you want to begin adding text.

   C Select a type layer and a shape layer; then choose Layer, Bind Type to Path.

   D You can't flow type along a vector path in Photoshop.

13 You're creating a logo based on text you've entered with the Type tool. You want to use the Direct Selection tool to reshape the characters to add visual interest. What must you do to the type layer before you can reshape the letters with the Direct Selection tool?

   A Choose Layer, Type, Convert to Shape.

   B Choose Layer, Rasterize, Type.

   C Choose Layer, New Layer Based Slice.

   D Choose Layer, Type, Warp Text.

14 How can you save a work path as a permanent path?

   A Specify a selection by using any selection tool; then choose Make Work Path from the Paths palette menu.

   B In the Paths palette, select the work path and click the "Load path as a selection" icon.

   C In the Paths palette, double-click the work path; then enter a new name and click OK.

   D In the Paths palette, select the work path and click the "Fill path with foreground color" button.

15 How can you convert a selection to a path?

   A Choose Select, Save Selection.

   B Choose Select, Load Selection.

   C In the Paths palette, click the "Load path as a selection" icon.

   D In the Paths palette, click the "Make work path from selection" icon.

U n i t   4

Creative image effects

Unit time: 70 minutes

Complete this unit, and you'll know how to:

A Use painting tools, filters, blending modes, and custom brushes to simulate illustrated and painted effects.

B Warp text and layers.

C Group layers and use Smart Objects when creating a composite.

D Apply filters as Smart Filters, and mask Smart Filters.

E Use the Layer Comps palette to create layer comps.

F Import, transform, and edit textures on 3D layers.

Topic A: Painted effects

This topic covers the following Adobe ACE exam objective for Photoshop CS3.

#	Objective
2.6	Create and edit a custom brush.

Filters and custom brushes

Explanation

In addition to adjusting photographic images to retain a realistic appearance, you can apply Photoshop's filters to make a photograph look more like a painting or sketch. You can use a filter along with blending modes to simulate the texture of a canvas or other painting surface, and you can create custom brushes for either "stamping" repeats of images or creating realistic-looking brush strokes.

To help simulate actual brush strokes and create a more realistic painting or sketch effect in an image, you might use the Art History Brush tool instead of a filter.

The History palette and the Art History Brush tool

You can paint in an image by dragging the History Brush tool or the Art History Brush tool. Rather than painting with solid color as you do with the Brush tool, however, you'll be painting with pixels from a state in the History palette.

History palette states and snapshots

The History palette records, by default, the 20 most recent actions you've performed in Photoshop. Each saved action is called a *state*. As you perform additional steps, older states are deleted from the History palette.

If you want to save the current image state so that it remains in the History palette no matter how many additional steps you perform, you can save it as a snapshot. A *snapshot* is a saved image state that appears at the top of the History palette. When you close the image, however, snapshots are cleared from the History palette.

To save the current image state as a named snapshot:

1 In the History palette, click the state that you want to save as a snapshot.
2 Open the New Snapshot dialog box by doing either of the following:
   - Press Alt and click the Create new snapshot button at the bottom of the History palette. (If you click this button without pressing Alt, the new snapshot is automatically named Snapshot 1. You can then double-click the name to change it.)
   - From the History palette menu, choose New Snapshot.
3 In the Name box, enter the name you want.
4 From the From list, select an option to specify whether the snapshot includes all document layers, the current layer, or all layers merged to a single layer.
5 Click OK.

Painting with the History Brush and Art History Brush tools

The History Brush tool paints pixels into an image exactly as they appear in the specified state or snapshot in the History palette. The Art History Brush tool paints the pixels from the specified history state but with a simulated painting style that you choose.

To paint pixels from a history state into the current image:

1 In the History palette, click to the left of the state or snapshot whose pixels you want to paint into the image, as shown in Exhibit 4-1.

2 In the toolbox, select the History Brush tool or the Art History Brush tool.

3 If you're using the Art History Brush tool, select the desired style from the Style list on the options bar.

4 Drag in the image to paint pixels from the specified history state.

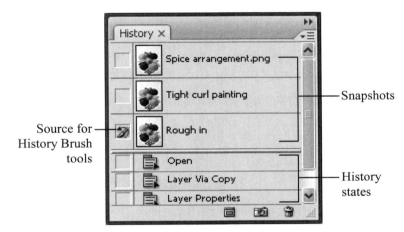

Exhibit 4-1: The History palette

Do it!

A-1: Simulating an illustration with the Art History Brush

Here's how	Here's why
1 Choose **Window**, **Workspace**, **Default Workspace**	To return all palettes to their original positions.
2 Open Spice arrangement	In the current unit folder.
Save the image in Photoshop format as **My spice painting**	
3 Press (CTRL) + (J)	To duplicate the Background layer. Ctrl+J is the keyboard shortcut for the Layer, New, Layer via Copy command.
Name the new layer **Painted**	
4 In the toolbox, click and hold	(The History Brush tool.) To display the tools grouped with the History Brush tool.
Select the **Art History Brush** tool	
From the Brush Preset picker, select the **Hard Round 5 pixels** brush	The third item in the list.
On the options bar, from the Style list, select **Tight Curl**	
Paint over the spices, using no more than five strokes	(Don't release the mouse button more than five times.) To create an abstract version of the image, based on the original.
5 Click	(The History palette icon in the collapsed dock of palettes.) To display the History palette.
6 Press (ALT) and click in the History palette	(The Create new snapshot button.) To open the New Snapshot dialog box.
In the Name box, enter **Tight Curl painting**	
Click **OK**	To save the snapshot.
7 In the History palette, click the **Layer Properties** state	To return to the original version of the image, with the Painted layer active.

8 Display the Brush Preset picker

Drag its bottom-right corner down and to the right

To display all of the brushes. This makes it easier to find a specific brush.

Select the indicated brush

The Dry Brush Tip Light Flow brush.

From the Style list, select **Dab**

On the options bar.

9 Paint over all of the spices

To rough in the color as a painter might.

Save this as a history state named **Rough in**

Press Alt and click the Create new snapshot button in the History palette, enter "Rough in," and click OK.

10 Display the Brush Preset picker and select the **Spatter 14 pixels** brush

11 Brush the spices from the center outward, leaving some edges from before, as shown

To return detail to the image. Because the target history state is the original painted version, it draws from a source that has more detail than you see in the current version.

Some edges will likely look unnatural where the two brushes meet. You'll blend in those edges with the History Brush.

12 Select the History Brush tool

From the Brush Preset picker, select the **Soft Round 45 pixels** brush

Using the History Brush tool, you will blend past brush strokes softly into the new ones.

13 Click to the left of the Rough in history state, as shown

(Near the top of the History palette.) To set the source from which the History Brush will draw. As you paint, you'll be painting the pixels from this history state.

14 Brush the areas between the spatter and rough-in strokes

15 Lower the opacity of the Painted
   layer to **85%**

To let the Background layer detail show through
a bit.

16 Update the image

Simulating a textured surface

Explanation

When you modify a photographic image to make it look like a painting or sketch, you might want to simulate the appearance of a textured surface. For example, you might want to make it appear that your image is painted onto a textured canvas. You can create a variety of textures by using the Texturizer filter.

If you apply the Texturizer filter directly to the layer containing your image pixels, the effect permanently changes those pixels. If you apply the texture to an additional layer, however, you can continually adjust how the image and the texture interact. To make the textured layer appear on the image pixels, apply the Overlay blending mode.

Using an Overlay-neutral color

In *Overlay blending mode*, middle gray is a neutral color. Pixels in the overlay layer that are darker than middle gray will darken the layer below, and pixels that are lighter than middle gray will lighten the layer below. Middle-gray pixels won't alter the appearance of the pixels in the layer below. When you apply a Texturizer filter to an Overlay blending-mode layer, the filter will darken and lighten parts of the underlying layers, creating an effect similar to applying the filter directly to the underlying layers.

Creating a texture effect by using Overlay mode

To create a texture effect by using Overlay mode:

1   Open the New Layer dialog box:
    - Press Alt and click the "Create a new layer" button.
    - From the Layers palette menu, choose New Layer.
2   In the Name box, enter a name for the new layer.
3   From the Mode list, select Overlay.
4   Check "Fill with Overlay-neutral color (50% gray)."
5   Click OK.
6   Choose Filter, Texture, Texturizer to open the Filter Gallery dialog box with the Texturizer options showing.
7   Specify the texture settings you want and click OK.

The texture won't appear over white or black pixels in the layer below. If you need to lighten or darken pixels in the layer below to convert white or black areas into light or dark gray so the texture appears in those areas, you can add a Levels adjustment layer above it. Drag the Output sliders to adjust the colors, and click OK.

Do it!

A-2: Blending a texture with Overlay mode

Here's how	Here's why
1 Press (ALT) and click 🔳 in the Layers palette	(The "Create a new layer" button.) To open the New Layer dialog box.
Name the layer **Canvas**	
From the Mode list, select **Overlay**	
Check **Fill with Overlay-neutral color (50% gray)**	
Click **OK**	A gray-filled layer appears in the Layers palette, but there is no effect on the image because in Overlay mode, gray is an invisible effect.
2 Choose **Filter**, **Texture**, **Texturizer...**	To open the Filter Gallery dialog box with the Texturizer settings showing.
Click **OK**	To use the default canvas texture.
3 Observe the image	

The canvas texture appears over the spices but not over the white background. Overlay mode won't add detail to white or black areas.

4 Select the Painted layer

You'll lower the Painted layer's contrast to make the surrounding areas gray in order to make the canvas texture visible in those areas.

Create a Levels adjustment layer

(In the Layers palette, click the "Create new fill or adjustment layer" button, and choose Levels from the pop-up menu.) The Levels dialog box opens.

Drag the white Output slider to **235**, as shown

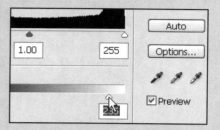

To change white pixels to light gray. The canvas texture now appears around the outside of the spices.

Click **OK**

To close the Levels dialog box.

5 Update and close the image

You'll reopen the image to verify that the history states and snapshots are all deleted.

6 Choose **File**, **Open Recent**, **My spice painting**

Observe that the history states you saved are gone

Close the image

Custom brushes

Explanation

You can create a brush from any image source up to 2500 × 2500 pixels. You can also specify whether the brush will create a continuous flow of paint or a series of "stamped" versions of the image.

To design a custom brush:

1   If you want the brush to have varying opacity levels, make the design either color or grayscale. The lighter the pixels in the original image, the less opaque those pixels will be within the brush.

2   Select the design with any selection tool. To create a hard-edged brush, set feathering to zero; to create soft edges, use higher feathering values.

3   Choose Edit, Define Brush Preset.

4   If you want to change brush settings—such as spacing, shape dynamics, and scattering—and save them as part of a preset, first select a brush tool and change the settings in the Brushes palette. Then, from the Brushes palette menu, choose New Brush Preset.

5   If you've changed settings and want to delete the original custom brush you created, click Brush Presets, and do either of the following:

- Press and hold Alt and click the original custom brush.
- Select the brush. Then either right-click it and choose Delete, or choose Delete Brush from the palette menu.

Do it!

A-3:   Creating a custom brush

Here's how	Here's why
1 Open Star anise	(From the current unit folder.) You'll create a custom brush from this star shape.
2 Select the Elliptical Marquee tool	
3 Create a circular marquee around the star shape, as shown	
	Press Alt as you drag from the center outward, and press Shift to constrain the marquee to a circular shape. Move the marquee, if necessary, by pressing the spacebar.
4 Choose **Edit, Define Brush Preset...**	To open the Brush Name dialog box.
In the Name box, enter **Star anise**	
Click **OK**	To create the preset. You'll now test the brush in a new image.

5 Create a 600px × 600px image with a white background, and name it **Star anise brush strokes**

Choose File, New; enter the file name; enter 600 in the Width and Height fields; select White from the Background Contents list; and click OK.

6 Select the Brush tool

Press ⒟

To set the foreground and background colors to their defaults of black and white.

From the Brush Preset picker, select the **Star anise** brush

The Star anise brush is the last item in the list.

Drag in the image to paint with the Star anise brush

The repetitions of the brush shape overlap one another and appear in grayscale, not in the original star anise colors. You'll change settings to make the brush appear to stamp individual repeats of the star anise, rather than creating overlapping ones that simulate smooth paint as you drag.

7 Save the image in the current unit folder

8 Display the Brushes palette

Select the **Brush Tip Shape** category

Drag the Spacing slider to a value of 120%

Any value over 100% creates individual "stamps" with space between them as you drag.

Drag to paint in the image

Next, you'll make the shapes vary in size and rotation as you drag.

9 Select the **Shape Dynamics** category

In the Brushes palette.

Drag the Size Jitter slider to a value of 25%

To vary the size automatically (not just according to pen pressure).

Drag the Angle Jitter slider to a value of 50%

To make the angle vary randomly.

Drag to paint in the image

The star anise stamp now varies in size and shape. You'll save these settings in a new preset.

10 From the Brushes palette menu, choose **New Brush Preset...**

To open the Brush Name dialog box.

In the Name box, enter **Star anise stamp**

Click **OK**

To create the preset. Next, you'll eliminate the original preset that created uniform overlapping stars.

11 Select the Brush Presets category

In the Brushes palette.

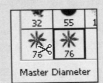

Press and hold (ALT) and point to the Star anise brush

To access the Delete cursor.

While still holding (ALT), click the Star anise brush

To delete it.

12 Update and close all images

Topic B: Warping

Explanation

You can reshape text, layer content, or selections by applying a *warp*. You can warp items to apply a variety of creative effects.

Warped text

You can warp Photoshop text to reshape it for a variety of effects. Warping text reshapes the text characters and flows the text along a curving baseline. After you apply a warp, the text remains editable as text. To warp text:

1 In the Layers palette, select the type layer.

2 Select the Horizontal Type tool or the Vertical Type tool.

3 On the options bar, click the Create warped text button to open the Warp Text dialog box.

4 From the Style list, select a warp style to preview its effect on the text in the selected layer. You can press Down Arrow to select each warp style in the list.

5 Select Horizontal or Vertical to specify the direction in which the style will affect the text.

6 Specify Bend, Horizontal Distortion, and Vertical Distortion values to control how the warp style will affect the text.

7 Click OK.

Do it!

B-1:   Warping text

Here's how	Here's why
1 Open Zesty	(In the current unit folder.) If a dialog box opens prompting you to update text layers, click Update.
Save the image as **My zesty**	
2 Select the Zesty! layer	In the Layers palette.
3 Select the Horizontal Type tool	
4 On the options bar, click [⬆]	(The Create warped text button.) To open the Warp Text dialog box.
5 From the Style list, select **Arc**	
Observe the text in the image	The text now flows along a curved baseline.
Press ⬇ several times to view each style	
6 From the Style list, select **Bulge**	
Set the Bend value to **+55**	
Set the Horizontal Distortion value to **-33**	
Set the Vertical Distortion value to **0**	If necessary.
7 Click **OK**	

Warping images

Explanation

You can also warp image content. You can warp a selection or an entire layer by applying a preset warp or creating a custom warp.

To warp a selection or layer:

1 Specify a selection, or select a layer in the Layers palette. (To select a layer, you can click it in the Layers palette, or press Ctrl and click any of the layer's content in the image window.)

2 Choose Edit, Transform, Warp to add a warp grid to the selection or layer.

3 Apply a preset warp, a custom warp, or both.

- Drag the grid handles to warp the selection.

- On the options bar, from the Warp list, select a preset warp. To further customize the preset warp effect, select Custom from the Warp list and drag the grid handles.

4 Press Enter.

You can use the Edit, Transform, Warp command and the Warp list on the options bar to apply a preset warp to a type layer. You cannot, however, apply a custom warp to a type layer.

Do it!

B-2: Warping image layers

Here's how	Here's why
1 Select the Move tool	
2 Press (CTRL) and click the red pepper in the image	To select the Red pepper layer. You'll experiment with unrealistic, cartoonish distortion of the red pepper to create a fun, playful image.
Press (CTRL) + (J)	To create a duplicate layer.
Name the layer **Red pepper warped**	
Hide the Red pepper, Red pepper shadow, and Pattern Fill 1 layers	
3 Choose **Edit, Transform, Warp**	A warp grid appears on the pepper.
On the options bar, from the Warp list, select **Fish**	To distort the pepper.
Drag the top-left handle of the grid down slightly, as shown	To adjust the curvature.
4 From the Warp list, select **Custom**	

5 Point in the grid handles as shown

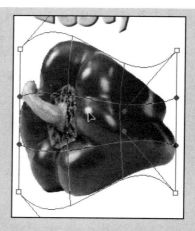

Notice that the mouse pointer changes shape.

Drag down and to the left, as shown

To further distort the image.

6 Drag the direction handle, extending from the top-right corner of the warp mesh, as shown

7 Press ⏎ ENTER   To complete the warp.

8 Choose **Edit, Transform, Warp**

A grid with even squares appears. You can't access a warp's original grid or clear an image warp after committing it.

Press ESC   To clear the grid.

9 Press (CTRL) and click the word **Zesty!** in the image	To select the type layer. You can apply or adjust a text warp by using the Edit, Transform, Warp command.
Choose **Edit, Transform, Warp**	Warp settings appear on the options bar.
Scrub the V value to **-12**	% V: [-12.0] %
	On the options bar.
10 On the options bar, click the Warp list	The Custom option is grayed out, indicating that you can't apply a custom warp to a type layer.
Press (↵ ENTER)	To complete the warp.
11 Update the image	

Topic C: Efficient compositing

This topic covers the following Adobe ACE exam objectives for Photoshop CS3.

#	Objective
3.1	Create and arrange layers and groups.
7.1	Create and use Smart Objects. (Smart Objects include: vector, raster, and camera raw files.)

Compositing

Explanation

When you create an image by combining multiple images—a process known as *compositing*—you can use several techniques to keep your workflow efficient. For example, you can group layers together to organize the Layers palette and to manipulate multiple layers as a unit. When you select a group, you can move all of its layers as a unit, or adjust the group's blending mode or opacity to apply those settings to all layers in the group. In addition, when applying transformations and other types of changes to layers, you can make those changes nondestructive by converting layers to Smart Objects. *Smart Objects* are objects that act as layers but store the original image data of one or more layers.

Grouping

When an image includes many layers, you might want to organize them into groups. A *group* is a container in the Layers palette that can store multiple layers. You can expand a group so all of its layers are listed in the Layers palette, or collapse the group to hide its list of layers.

To create an empty group with the default settings, click the "Create a new group" button in the Layers palette. The group will be named Group 1.

To create an empty group with settings you specify:

1   Open the New Group dialog box by doing either of the following:
    • From the Layers palette menu, choose New Group.
    • Press Alt and click the "Create a new group" button.
2   In the Name box, enter a name for the group.
3   Specify a color for the group icon, and specify a blending mode and opacity for the group.
4   Click OK.

To create a group containing selected layers and using the default settings:

1   Select the layers you want to store in the group.
2   Drag the selected layers to the "Create a new group" button. The group will be named Group 1.

To create a group containing selected layers and using settings you specify:

1   Select the layers you want to store in the group.

2   Open the New Group from Layers dialog box:
   - From the Layers palette menu, choose New Group from Layers.
   - Press Alt and drag the layers to the "Create a new group" button.

3   In the Name box, enter a name for the group.

4   Specify a color for the group icon, and specify a blending mode and opacity for the group.

5   Click OK.

To add a layer to a group in the Layers palette, drag the desired layer onto the group. To delete a group, select it and click the Delete layer button. In the alert dialog box that appears, click Group and Contents to delete the group and its layers, or click Group Only to delete the group without deleting the layers within it.

Do it!

C-1: Grouping layers

Here's how	Here's why
1 Hide the Red pepper warped layer	
Show the Red pepper and Red pepper shadow layers	
2 Select the Red pepper layer	
Press (SHIFT) and click the Chiles shadow layer	To select the range of layers.
3 From the Layers palette menu, choose **New Group from Layers...**	To open the New Group from Layers dialog box.
In the Name box, enter **Vegetables**	
Click **OK**	To create the group.
4 Verify that the Vegetables group is selected	
Using the Move tool, drag in the image	To move all layers in the group at once.
Press (CTRL) + (Z)	To undo the move.
5 Reduce the opacity of the Vegetables group to **50%**	Observe that all of the layers in the group change opacity.
Choose **Edit**, **Undo Master Opacity Change**	To return the group to 100% opacity.

Smart Objects

Explanation

Transforming image content, such as by rotating, scaling, or warping, is typically a destructive edit. A *destructive edit* is one that permanently changes pixel data. Therefore, transforming an image can degrade image quality. For example, if you scale a layer down to 25% of its initial size, the layer contents are rendered at that smaller size, re-creating the layer contents with fewer pixels. If you later scale the layer back to its original size, it will likely appear with significant blurring.

You can transform image content nondestructively by converting it to a Smart Object. A *Smart Object* stores the original image data and references it each time you apply a transformation. Therefore, you can transform a Smart Object, and each time, it's as though you're transforming the original image data, as shown in Exhibit 4-2.

Transformed layer content   Transformed Smart Object

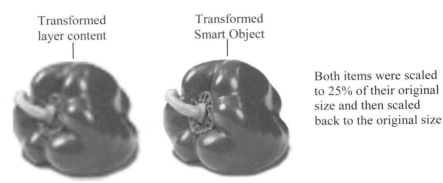

Both items were scaled to 25% of their original size and then scaled back to the original size

Exhibit 4-2: Transformed layer content compared to a transformed Smart Object

Converting layers to Smart Objects

You can convert one or more layers to a single Smart Object. In the Layers palette, a Smart Object looks like a layer, but its thumbnail has a Smart Object badge icon.

To convert layers to a Smart Object, select the layer or layers you want to convert, and choose Convert to Smart Object from the Layers palette menu. The layers appear as a single Smart Object in the Layers palette, and the Smart Object badge appears on the thumbnail.

After converting a layer or layers to a Smart Object, you can transform the Smart Object without cumulatively degrading the image with each new transformation.

C-2: Creating and transforming Smart Objects

Here's how	Here's why
1 In the Layers palette, click as shown	
	Click the small gray arrow to the left of the Vegetables group icon to expand the Vegetables group.
Select the Red pepper and Red pepper shadow layers	Click the Red pepper layer; then Shift+click to select the Red pepper shadow layer.
2 From the Layers palette menu, choose **Convert to Smart Object**	To convert the two layers into a single Smart Object.
Observe the badge on the Smart Object thumbnail	
	The object appears as one layer.
3 Convert the Garlic and Garlic shadow layers to a Smart Object	Select the Garlic and Garlic shadow layers, and choose Convert to Smart Object from the Layers palette menu.
Convert the Chiles and Chiles shadow layers into a Smart Object	
4 In the Layers palette, select the **Red pepper** Smart Object	
Press (SHIFT) and click the **Chiles** Smart Object	To select all three Smart Objects.
5 Choose **Edit**, **Free Transform**	To show the transformation handles in the image.
Widen the image window	If necessary.

6 Press (SHIFT) and drag the bottom-right transform handle up and to the left

(Don't release the mouse button.) To reduce the size of the selected objects proportionally.

When the W and H values on the options bar are about 50%, release the mouse button

Press (↵ ENTER)

To complete the transformation.

7 In the Layers palette, select each Smart Object individually, and position the objects as shown

8 Select the Garlic layer

Press (CTRL) + (T)

(Or choose Edit, Free Transform.) You'll rescale the garlic image.

Scale the image to approximately **60%**

(Drag the selection handles.) To enlarge it from its original scale value of 50%.

9 Select the Chiles layer

Scale it to approximately **75%**

Press Ctrl+T to free-transform the image.

Rotate the Chiles layer slightly counterclockwise

Choose Edit, Transform, Rotate. Point to just outside the bottom-right corner selection handle, and drag up slightly. Press Enter.

10 Rearrange the three Smart Objects to their positions in Step 7

11 Update the file

Smart Object contents

Explanation

After converting one or more layers or other content to a Smart Object, you can still access and modify the original content. In addition, you can export the Smart Object content as a separate file.

Modifying Smart Object contents

If you convert three layers to a single Smart Object, you can still access the three original layers in a separate image window and make changes that will be reflected in the Smart Object.

To modify the original content:

1 In the Layers palette, select the Smart Object.
2 From the Layers palette menu, choose Edit Contents. A message box appears, explaining that after changing the Smart Object's contents, you'll have to save them to update the Smart Object.
3 Click OK. The original content that you converted to a Smart Object appears in a new window.
4 Modify the content, and then choose File, Save.
5 Close the window displaying the edited content to return to the original image window. This window now displays the updated Smart Object content.

Exporting Smart Object contents

You might want to export Smart Object content as a separate file so you can use it in other images. To do so, right-click a Smart Object in the Layers palette, and choose Export Contents from the shortcut menu. In the Save dialog box that opens, enter a name for the exported content, and click Save.

The image is exported as a Smart Object file, which uses the PSB file format. You can place the file in other image files as a Smart Object, or you can open it directly in its own image window.

Do it!

C-3: Working with Smart Object contents

Here's how	Here's why
1 Select the Chiles layer	You'll change the shadow of the chiles to better match the shadows of the other vegetables.
From the Layers palette menu, choose **Edit Contents**	A dialog box appears, indicating that you must choose File, Save to commit your changes after editing the content.
Click **OK**	The chiles and shadow appear in a separate image window.
2 Select the Chiles shadow layer	
With the Move tool selected, press ⬇ four times	To increase the distance between the chiles and the shadow.
3 Choose **File**, **Save**	
Close the image	The chiles' shadow more closely matches the shadows of the other vegetables. Next, you'll export the Red pepper and its shadow so that you can use it in other images.
4 Right-click the Red pepper layer	To display the shortcut menu.
Choose **Export Contents...**	To open the Save dialog box. Note that the file type is PSB. A PSB file can be placed in other images.
Click **Save**	To export the object.
5 Update the image	

Vector Smart Objects

Explanation

Smart Objects can also store vector data. If you place an Illustrator file into a Photoshop image, the file is placed as a Smart Object, maintaining the original vector data. Therefore, you can transform and manipulate the placed vector file without having to rasterize it. In addition, because vector images can be scaled up without any loss of image quality or crispness, you can safely scale a vector Smart Object larger than its original size.

To place a vector file into an image as a Smart Object:

1 Choose File, Place to open the Place dialog box.
2 Select the vector file you want to place, and click Place. The Place PDF dialog box appears.
3 Click OK, and press Enter to display the placed content as a Smart Object.

You can right-click a Smart Object based on an Illustrator file and choose Edit Contents to open the file in Adobe Illustrator, if you have that software on your computer.

Do it!

C-4: Creating vector Smart Objects

Here's how	Here's why
1 Select the Zesty! layer	You'll place an Illustrator file above the Zesty! layer.
Choose **File, Place...**	To open the Place dialog box.
Select **Outlander logo**	
Click **Place**	The Place PDF dialog box appears.
2 In the Crop To list, select **Art Box**	
Click **OK**	To place the logo.
Press (↵ ENTER)	To commit the change. You'll be able to continually transform this Smart Object without degrading the image quality.
3 Scale the logo to about **30%** Place it below and to the right of the vegetables, as shown	

4 Move the objects to the right, as shown

5 Select the logo

   Press ⌈ CTRL ⌉ + ⌈ T ⌉   To allow you to free-transform the logo.

6 Rotate and resize as shown

When you place vector art, it's treated as a Smart Object. Therefore, it scales smoothly instead of appearing pixilated, as it would if it were rasterized and resized to over twice its original size.

7 Using the Crop tool, crop the image as shown

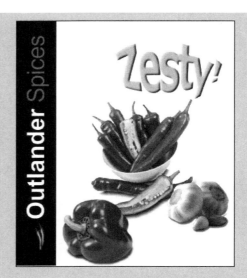

8 Show the Pattern Fill 1 layer

9 Update the image

10 Close the image

Topic D: Smart Filters

This topic covers the following Adobe ACE exam objective for Photoshop CS3.

#	Objective
7.2	Convert content to be used with Smart Filters. (Options include: applying filters, masking filters, and editing and deleting filters.)

Nondestructive filters

Explanation

When you apply a filter to an image, the filter changes the pixel data to which it is applied. However, you can apply a filter as a *Smart Filter* so that it is applied nondestructively. You can then experiment with filter settings without destructively changing the actual image pixel data. Therefore, you can easily modify a filter's effects, or you can remove the filter altogether to return the image to its original appearance.

If you want to apply a filter to a layer as a Smart Filter, you must first convert the layer to a Smart Object layer. You can then apply almost any Photoshop filter to the Smart Object layer, and it will be applied as a Smart Filter. You can also apply the Shadow/Highlight and Variations adjustments as Smart Filters. However, you can't apply the following filters as Smart Filters:

- Extract
- Liquefy
- Pattern Maker
- Vanishing Point

Apply a Smart Filter

If the layer to which you want to apply a Smart Filter is not already a Smart Object layer, then select the layer and choose Filter, Convert for Smart Filters. To apply a Smart Filter, select a Smart Object layer, choose a filter, and specify its settings. The Smart Filter then appears in the Layers palette, as shown in Exhibit 4-3.

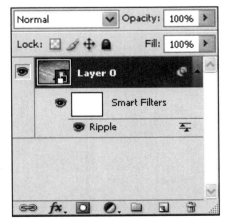

Exhibit 4-3: The Ripple filter applied as a Smart Filter to a Smart Object layer

Edit a Smart Filter

After you apply a Smart Filter, you can edit its effects at any time. Each time you adjust the filter settings, the new settings are applied to the original image data, because the Smart Filter is applied nondestructively. To edit a Smart Filter's settings, double-click it in the Layers palette to open the filter's dialog box.

Remove a Smart Filter

If you want to remove a Smart Filter, drag it to the Delete layer button in the Layers palette. The Smart Filter will be removed and its effects will no longer apply to the image.

Do it!

D-1: Applying Smart Filters

Here's how	Here's why
1 Open Puppy	In the current unit folder.
2 Save the image in Photoshop format as **My puppy**	The image contains a single layer. You'll convert the layer to a Smart Object so you can apply filters as Smart Filters.
3 Choose **Filter**, **Convert for Smart Filters**	A dialog box informs you that the layer will be converted to a Smart Object.
Click **OK**	The layer icon displays a badge to indicate that it is a Smart Object layer. You can now apply filters as Smart Filters.
4 Choose **Filter**, **Distort**, **Ripple...**	To open the Ripple dialog box.
5 Drag the Amount slider to approximately **400** From the Size list, select **Large** Click **OK**	
	The Smart Filter applies to the entire image. Because you applied this filter as a Smart Filter, you can adjust its settings at any time, and the changes will be based on the original image, rather than on the current filtered version of the image. Therefore, you can regain earlier image detail that the filter might have obscured.

6 Double-click **Ripple** as shown

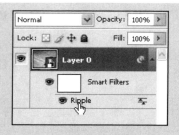

To open the Ripple dialog box.

Drag the Amount slider to
approximately **150**

Click **OK**

More of the original image detail returns. You'll
add a second Smart Filter.

7 Choose **Filter**, **Texture**,
Patchwork...

To open the Filter Gallery dialog box,
displaying the Patchwork settings.

Click **OK**

Both Smart Filters are now listed in the Layers
palette. You'll remove the Smart Filter you just
added.

8 Drag the Patchwork Smart Filter
to the Delete layer button

(In the Layers palette.) To delete the Smart
Filter. The Smart Filter is deleted, and its effects
no longer apply to the image.

9 Update the image

Smart Filter masks

Explanation

One of the benefits of Smart Filters is that you can easily mask their effects to control which portion of the image displays the filter effects, and you can edit the mask as often as necessary. When you apply a Smart Filter to a Smart Object, a mask thumbnail appears on the Smart Filters line in the Layers palette. By default, the mask thumbnail is white, indicating that the filter's effects will appear on the entire layer. You can work with filter masks by using the same techniques you use to work with layer masks. For example, you can paint with black on a filter mask to hide the filter's effects.

Before you apply a Smart Filter, you can select a portion of a Smart Object layer so that when you apply the Smart Filter, it will automatically create a filter mask based on the selection. The filter mask thumbnail will use white to indicate areas where the filter effect will appear, and use black to indicate areas where the effect won't appear.

D-2: Masking Smart Filter effects

Here's how	Here's why
1 Click the Smart Filters mask thumbnail as shown	
	To select the mask thumbnail so you can edit the mask by using painting tools. You'll paint with black to hide the Smart Filter everywhere except on the puppy.
2 Select the Brush tool	
3 Press ⓧ	To switch the foreground and background colors so that black is now the foreground color.
4 Display the Brush Preset picker	
Select a soft round brush of any size	
Drag the Master Diameter slider to approximately **400**	
5 Drag throughout the image, except on the puppy	To apply black to the filter mask so that the filter's effect is apparent only on the puppy and slightly around it.
6 Observe the filter mask thumbnail	
	The thumbnail is black in the areas around the puppy where you painted. The thumbnail is white in only the area of the image where the puppy appears, so only that part will display the filter's effects.
7 Hide and show the Smart Filters' effects	Click the eye icon next to Smart Filters in the layers palette.
8 Update and close the image	

Topic E: Layer comps

This topic covers the following Adobe ACE exam objective for Photoshop CS3.

#	Objective
3.2	Explain the purpose of layer comps and when you would use a layer comp.

The Layer Comps palette

Explanation

When you're preparing an image that other people will review and approve, you'll probably want to create several versions of it. Multiple versions of a design or layout are typically called *comps*, which is short for *compositions*. You can use Photoshop to generate multiple comps in a single image file.

You can use the Layer Comps palette to store multiple comps of an image. Each layer comp is basically a snapshot of the Layers palette in a specified state. A layer comp stores three types of layer data for each layer:

- Layer visibility
- The position of layer content in the image
- The layer's appearance (style and blending mode)

Creating layer comps

To create a layer comp:

1 Specify the layer options that you want to use to control the appearance of the image for the comp.

2 Choose Window, Layer Comps, or activate the Layer Comps tab in the palette well, to open the Layer Comps palette.

3 At the bottom of the palette, click the Create New Layer Comp button to open the New Layer Comp dialog box.

4 Enter a name for the comp, specify the Layers palette options you want the comp to record, and click OK.

Viewing layer comps

After creating layer comps, you can click to the left of their names in the Layer Comps palette to view them, as shown in Exhibit 4-4. You can also click the Apply Next and Apply Previous buttons to cycle through the layer comps.

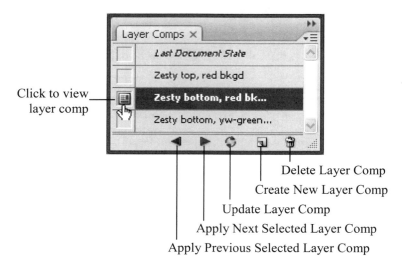

Click to view layer comp

Delete Layer Comp
Create New Layer Comp
Update Layer Comp
Apply Next Selected Layer Comp
Apply Previous Selected Layer Comp

Exhibit 4-4: The Layer Comps palette

Modifying layer comps

Changes you make in an image while viewing a layer comp do not automatically update the layer comp itself. To modify a layer comp:

1   In the Layer Comps palette, select the layer comp you want to change.
2   Make your changes in the image.
3   In the Layer Comps palette, click the Update Layer Comp button.

Exporting layer comps

You can export layer comps as separate files. This is useful when you want to show the layer comps to a client. To export layer comps:

1   Choose File, Scripts.
2   From the Scripts submenu, choose the type of document that you want to export the comps to:
    • Choose Layer Comps To Files if you want to create an individual image file for each comp.
    • Choose Layer Comps to PDF if you want to create a single PDF file that displays the comps as a slide show.
    • Choose Layer Comps to WPG if you want to export the comps as a Web page gallery.
3   Specify a name for the comps, and click Run.
4   When the conversion is complete, click OK.

Do it!

E-1:   Creating layer comps

Here's how	Here's why
1 Open My zesty	
2 Click 🖼	(The Layer Comps palette icon in the collapsed dock of palettes.) To display the Layer Comps palette.
Click 🔲	(The Create New Layer Comp button.) To open the New Layer Comp dialog box.
In the Name box, enter **Zesty top**, **red bkgd**	
Check all three check boxes	
Click **OK**	To close the dialog box.
3 Switch the positions of the vegetables and **Zesty!** items in the image, as shown	

Create a layer comp called **Zesty bottom**, **red bkgd**	In the Layer Comps palette, click the Create New Layer Comp button. Enter the comp name and click OK.
4 Double-click the Pattern Fill 1 layer	To open the Layer Style dialog box.
Click **Color Overlay**	To display the Color Overlay settings.
Click the color swatch to the right of the Blend Mode list	To open the Color Picker dialog box.
Set the color to **255** Red, **255** Green, **0** Blue	To specify a bright yellow color.
Close the Color Picker and the Layer Style dialog box	

5 Double-click the Zesty layer   To open the Layer Style dialog box.

   Click **Gradient Overlay**   To display the Gradient Overlay settings.

   From the Gradient list, select
   Violet, Orange

   Click **OK**

To return to the image.

6 Create a layer comp named
   Zesty bottom, **yw-green
   bkgd**

7 In the Layer Comps palette, click   To switch between the comps.
   the box to the left of each layer
   comp

8 In the "Zesty top, red bkgd" layer
   comp, move **Zesty!** slightly to
   the left

   View another layer comp, and   The word "Zesty" is back in its original position.
   then return to the "Zesty top, red
   bkgd" layer comp

9 Move **Zesty!** slightly to the left   In the "Zesty top, red bkgd" layer comp.

   In the Layer Comps palette, click   (The Update Layer Comp button) To update the
   [icon]   "Zesty top, red bkgd" layer comp with the
   change.

   Next, you'll make a PDF file to give to a client,
   with each option on a separate page.

10 Choose **File**, **Scripts**, **Layer Comps to PDF...**	To open the Layer Comps To PDF dialog box.
Click **Browse**	To open the Select Destination dialog box.
Navigate to the current unit folder	
In the File name box, enter **Zesty comps**	
Click **Save**	To return to the Layer Comps To PDF dialog box.
11 Click **Run**	
In the Script Alert dialog box, click **OK**	
12 In Windows Explorer, navigate to the current unit folder	
Open Zesty comps	A dialog box might appear, asking whether you want to open the document in full screen mode.
Click **Yes**	(If necessary.) Adobe Reader starts, and a slide show displays each layer comp.
When the slide show ends, press (ESC)	To display the Adobe Reader menu bar and tools.
13 Close Adobe Reader	
Close Windows Explorer	
14 Update and close all images	In Photoshop.

Topic F: 3D layers

This topic covers the following Adobe ACE exam objective for Photoshop CS3.

#	Objective
7.4	Import, transform, and edit textures on 3D layers.

3D content in Photoshop CS3 Extended

Explanation

The Photoshop CS3 Extended application supports 3D files. You can open and work with 3D files created in such programs as Adobe Acrobat 3D, 3D Studio Max, Alias, Maya, and Google Earth. The file formats supported are .u3d, .3ds, .obj, .kmz, and Collide.

Open or place 3D files

You can open a 3D file in Photoshop CS3 Extended by using the File, Open command. If you want to add a 3D file to an existing Photoshop file, then choose Layer, 3D Layers, New Layer From 3D file.

Transform 3D layers

You can use the 3D tools in Photoshop CS3 Extended to move or scale a 3D model, adjust lighting, or change render modes, such as by changing from solid to wireframe mode. However, you must use a 3D authoring program to edit the 3D model itself.

To access the 3D tools, you must switch to 3D transform mode. To do so, do either of the following:

- In the Layers palette, double-click the 3D layer thumbnail.
- Choose Layer, 3D Layers, Transform 3D Model.

In 3D transform mode, the 3D tools appear on the options bar, as shown in Exhibit 4-5. While you work in 3D transform mode, you cannot access other Photoshop functions or menu commands. To exit 3D transform mode, do either of the following:

- To keep your changes, click the Commit 3D Transform button on the options bar or press Enter.
- To remove your changes, click the Cancel 3D Transform button on the options bar or press Esc.

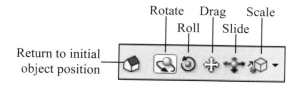

Exhibit 4-5: The 3D transform tools

The 3D tools are described in the following table.

Item	Description
Return to initial object position	Click to remove the 3D transforms applied, returning the 3D object to its original position, size, and rotation.
Rotate	Drag up or down to rotate the 3D object around its x-axis, or drag right or left to rotate it around its y-axis.
Roll	Drag left or right to rotate the 3D object around its z-axis.
Drag	Drag to reposition the 3D object.
Slide	Drag left or right to move the 3D object, drag down to move the object closer, or drag up to move it farther away.
Scale	Drag up to make the 3D object larger, or drag down to make the 3D object smaller.

3D layer textures

When you add 3D content to an image in Photoshop CS3 Extended, the 3D model is placed on a 3D layer, as shown in Exhibit 4-6. If the 3D file includes one or more textures, the textures are listed in the Layers palette below the 3D layer. A texture layer is added as a 2D layer. Although you can't create new textures for 3D content in Photoshop, you can edit the textures with Photoshop's painting and adjustment tools.

To edit textures for 3D content:

1 In the Layers palette, double-click the texture you want to edit. The texture opens in a separate document window.
2 Use any of Photoshop's tools to paint or edit the texture just as you'd paint or edit any Photoshop image.
3 Save the texture document. If the 3D file is a non-Photoshop format, then choose Layer, 3D Layers, Replace Textures after you edit the texture file.

You can click the eye icon for an individual texture layer or for the top-level texture layer to prevent textures from being displayed on the 3D model.

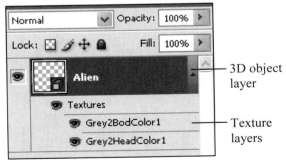

Exhibit 4-6: 3D content in the Layers palette

Do it!

F-1: Discussing 3D support in Photoshop CS3 Extended

Questions and answers

1 How can you get 3D content into Photoshop CS3 Extended?

2 What must you do before you can use Photoshop's editing tools to edit a texture for a 3D object?

3 Which 3D transform tool should you use to rotate a 3D object around its z-axis?

4 How can you rotate a 3D object around its x-axis or y-axis?

5 You must use a 3D authoring program to edit a 3D model itself. What types of actions can you perform with 3D objects in Photoshop CS3 Extended?

Unit summary: Creative image effects

Topic A In this topic, you used the **Art History Brush tool** to simulate a painted effect. You also applied a **Texturizer filter** to an Overlay blending-mode layer to simulate a textured surface. Finally, you created a **custom brush preset** from a pixel area in an image.

Topic B In this topic, you used the Create Warped Text button to **warp** a type layer. You also used the Edit, Transform, Warp command to apply a preset warp and to customize a warp.

Topic C In this topic, you **grouped layers** and manipulated them. In addition, you converted layers to **Smart Objects** and transformed them. You also modified the contents of Smart Objects and exported them. Finally, you placed a vector file as a Smart Object.

Topic D In this topic, you converted a layer to a Smart Object, and then you applied a filter as a **Smart Filter**. You also applied a mask to a Smart Filter.

Topic E In this topic, you used the Layer Comps palette to create **layer comps**. You also viewed and modified layer comps. Finally, you exported layer comps.

Topic F In this topic, you learned how to open and import **3D objects** in Photoshop CS3 Extended. You also learned how to transform 3D objects and edit textures for 3D objects.

Independent practice activity

In this activity, you'll group layers and convert layer contents to Smart Objects. You'll create layer comps, and you'll paint with the Art History Brush.

1 Open Granular spices, located in the current unit folder, and save the image as **My granular spices**.

2 Group the spice and shadow layers for each spice into one new group named **Spices**. (*Hint*: Select the layers and choose New Group from Layers from the Layers palette menu.)

3 Convert each pair (a spice and its shadow) to a Smart Object. Resize them as desired, but don't enlarge past 100%. (*Hint*: Expand the Spices group. Select each pair, and choose Convert to Smart Object from the Layers palette menu. Select each Smart Object, press Ctrl+T, and resize.)

4 Place Outlander logo. Put it at the top-left corner of the image at 35% size. (*Hint*: Choose File, Place, and select the Outlander logo from the current unit folder. Be sure to commit the resizing and repositioning actions when you're done.)

5 In a separate step, transform the logo to 60% size, as shown in Exhibit 4-7.

6 Save a layer comp named **Logo top left**. (*Hint*: Click the Create New Layer Comp button in the Layer Comps palette.)

7 Move the Outlander logo to the bottom-right corner of the image, and save a layer comp named **Logo bottom right**.

8 Choose **Image, Duplicate**; name the image **My granular spices painting**; and save it.

9 Delete the Outlander logo layer and then flatten the image. (*Hint*: These commands are in the Layers palette menu.)

10 In the History palette, set the Flatten Image state as the source for the History Brush tool. (*Hint*: Click the column to the left of the Flatten Image state so that the History Brush tool icon appears there.)

11 Paint with the Art History Brush tool to make the image look as though it were painted, as shown in Exhibit 4-8. (*Hint*: Try using a Soft Round 13-pixel brush.)

12 Update and close all images.

Exhibit 4-7: The image as it appears after Step 5 in the independent practice activity

Exhibit 4-8: The image as it appears after Step 11

Review questions

1 Which tools paint in the image based on the information in image states? [Choose all that apply.]

   A History Brush

   B Clone Stamp

   C Patch

   D Art History Brush

2 In a layer with Overlay mode applied, what color will appear perfectly transparent to the underlying layer?

3 Of the following statements about the selected area you use to define a custom brush, which are true? [Choose all that apply.]

   A The selection must be perfectly square.

   B The selection must be rectangular.

   C The selection can be any shape.

   D You can apply a feather to the selection to create a soft-edged brush.

4 How can you create a custom brush based on the current selection?

   A Choose Edit, Define Brush Preset.

   B Choose Edit, Define Pattern.

   C Choose Edit, Preset Manager.

   D Choose Edit, Assign Profile.

5 True or false: After you apply a warp to type, the text remains editable.

6 Which can you apply to a selection or layer? [Choose all that apply.]

   A A preset warp.

   B A custom warp.

   C A preset warp and a custom warp at the same time.

   D None; you can apply a warp only to an entire layer, not to a selection.

7 To organize layers so they appear in a collapsible layer with a folder icon, you should:

   A Link them.

   B Group them.

   C Create a clipping mask.

   D Combine them into a Smart Object.

8 Which of the following statements are true? [Choose all that apply.]

    A A Smart Object can be transformed to a small size and then back to its original size with no loss of quality.

    B A Smart Object's data cannot be edited after you've converted it from layer data.

    C Only raster, not vector, data can be stored as a Smart Object.

    D You can combine multiple layers into one Smart Object.

9 How can you convert several selected layers into a Smart Object?

    A From the Layers palette menu, choose New Group.

    B From the Layers palette menu, choose Convert to Smart Object.

    C From the Layers palette menu, choose New Group from Layers.

    D From the Layers palette menu, choose Merge Layers.

10 You want to apply a filter to a layer nondestructively. What must you do first?

    A Convert the layer to a 3D object layer.

    B Convert the layer to a background layer.

    C Convert the layer to a Smart Object layer.

    D Convert the layer to an adjustment layer.

11 You've applied the Mezzotint filter as a Smart Filter, and you want to change the filter settings. How can you open the dialog box to change the filter settings?

    A Double-click the Mezzotint layer in the Layers palette.

    B Choose Filter, Pixelate, Mezzotint.

    C Choose Filter, Mezzotint.

    D Double-click the Smart Filters layer in the Layers palette.

12 What types of layer data can vary among layer comps for a single layer? [Choose all that apply.]

    A Layer visibility

    B Pixel content

    C The position of layer content in the image

    D The layer blending mode

13 From which submenu can you export layer comps?

    A File, Automate

    B File, Scripts

    C File, Export

    D File, Place

14 You want to add a 3D object to an image you've created in Photoshop CS3 Extended. How should you open the 3D object?

    A Choose File, Open.

    B Choose File, Place.

    C Choose Layer, 3D Layers, New Layer From 3D file.

    D Choose it from the File, Import submenu.

15 You want to change the color of a texture for a 3D layer. What must you do before you can edit the texture layer?

    A Click the texture layer in the Layers palette.

    B Double-click the 3D layer thumbnail icon in the Layers palette.

    C Choose Layer, 3D Layers, New Layer From 3D file.

    D Double-click the texture layer in the Layers palette.

Unit 5

Video

Unit time: 50 minutes

Complete this unit, and you'll know how to:

A Prepare images for use in video productions.

B Open QuickTime video content in video layers, and edit video-frame content.

Topic A: Images for video

This topic covers the following Adobe ACE exam objectives for Photoshop CS3.

#	Objective
5.1	Given a scenario, create a new document by selecting the appropriate document preset.
5.2	Explain the purpose of Video Preview.
5.3	Describe the purpose of pixel aspect ratio correction.
1.3	Given a scenario, select the appropriate color mode for an image. (Scenarios include for Web, Video, Print, and Mobile.)

Preparing images for video

Explanation

Many video productions include still images along with motion elements. Properly preparing images for video involves considerations different from those used for images for print or for the Web.

Pixel aspect ratio

Computer monitors display images with square pixels. However, video monitors, such as televisions, use rectangular pixels. For example, the *NTSC video standard*—used in North America, Japan, Korea, and Mexico—displays pixels that are approximately 90% as wide as they are tall, as shown in Exhibit 5-1. Therefore, the *pixel aspect ratio* (the width of a pixel relative to its height) for NTSC is 0.9. The PAL standard, used in Europe, also uses rectangular pixels, but ones that are wider than they are tall (with a pixel aspect ratio of 1.066).

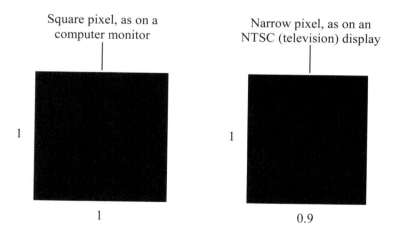

Exhibit 5-1: NTSC video has a 0.9 pixel aspect ratio

This difference in pixel width means that images that look correct on your computer monitor will appear distorted horizontally when imported into a video application, such as Adobe Premiere. For example, if you create the image shown in Exhibit 5-2 as a standard Photoshop image, it will appear too narrow when used in an NTSC video.

Image as it appears on a
computer monitor

Image as it appears on an
NTSC (television) monitor

Exhibit 5-2: A standard Photoshop image will appear distorted in a video production

Photoshop can help you counteract this problem in two ways. First, Photoshop can display images on a video monitor that's connected to your computer via a FireWire interface. Choose File, Export, Video Preview to choose output options before sending the image to the display, or choose File, Export, Send Video Preview to Device to view it immediately.

Second, Photoshop allows you to view images with a non-square pixel aspect ratio so you can use your computer monitor to simulate the display of a video monitor. To choose a pixel aspect ratio to display, choose Image, Pixel Aspect Ratio and select a video standard. Photoshop will retain the number of pixels in the image, but will adjust the width of the image's display based on the selected pixel aspect ratio. Because pixel aspect ratio correction doesn't offer an exact representation of the image pixels, however, you should turn it off to see the image at the highest quality setting.

Do it!

A-1:   Viewing an image with a non-square pixel aspect ratio

Here's how	Here's why
1 Open DVD title image	This image was designed with square pixels, not taking into account the pixel aspect ratio of NTSC video, for which the image was intended.
2 Observe the shape of the dish	The dish appears almost perfectly circular.
3 Choose **Image**, **Pixel Aspect Ratio**, **D1/DV NTSC (0.9)**	To display the image as it would appear in a video shown on a television.
4 Observe the shape of the dish	The dish appears narrower than it should.
5 Choose **Image**, **Pixel Aspect Ratio**, **Square**	To return the image to its original appearance.

Video format presets

When you create an image, you can select a standard video format preset. In addition to setting the image dimensions, the preset sets the color mode to 8-bit RGB (as it should be for video), sets the pixel aspect ratio to match the format, and generates guides for *safe zones*.

Safe zones

Television sets overscan, or enlarge, the images they receive, so pixels at the edges won't appear. The amount of overscan varies with individual sets, so you should avoid positioning important details close to the edges.

Video professionals typically consider approximately 90% of the image to be within the *action-safe* zone, where motion critical to understanding the video should remain. Because text is usually more important than movement, professionals recommend keeping text within a *title-safe* zone of about 80% of the frame size. The guides Photoshop creates for video format presets represent the action- and title-safe zones, as shown in Exhibit 5-3.

Exhibit 5-3: Action- and title-safe zones

Video preset image dimensions

Although there are several television resolution standards, the most common aspect ratio for television screens is 4:3—the image is four units wide and three units high. The DV NTSC standard is 480 scan lines (which equate to image pixels) tall. If televisions used square pixels, the image would be 640 × 480 (because 640/480 = 4/3). However, because the display pixels are narrow, the DV (digital video) standard specifies a resolution of 720 × 480.

Working with video preset images

One of the advantages of working with a video preset image is that new items you create will look right with the pixel aspect correction applied. For example, if you hold the Shift key as you drag an elliptical shape, it will look circular as you intended, not stretched horizontally (even though it's created with a different number of horizontal and vertical pixels to compensate for the non-square pixels). Similarly, when you create text with pixel aspect ratio correction turned on, the text is automatically scaled horizontally so it looks correct on screen and in the video application in which you place the image.

Do it!   **A-2: Creating an image for video**

Here's how	Here's why
1 Press ⟨D⟩	(If necessary.) To set the foreground and background colors to the defaults of black and white.
Press ⟨X⟩	To switch the foreground and background colors so the background is black. You want the background of the new file to be black.
2 Choose **File**, **New...**	To open the New dialog box.
3 In the Name box, enter **DVD menu**	This image will contain the title, image, and navigation elements for a DVD.
4 From the Preset list, select **Film & Video**	
Verify that NTSC DV is selected in the Size list	The video is in DV format.
5 From the Background Contents list, select **Background Color**	To set the background color to black.
Click **OK**	To close the New dialog box. Photoshop might open another dialog box, explaining that you should turn off pixel aspect ratio correction for maximum image quality.
Click **OK**	(If necessary.) To close the dialog box.
6 Show the rulers	Choose View, Rulers, if necessary.

7   Select the Horizontal Type tool

     You'll specify certain text formatting and then create some text within the title-safe zone.

     Click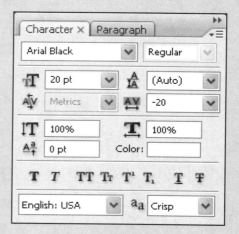

     (On the options bar.) To open the Character palette.

     Specify the formatting options indicated

     The font should be Arial Black, Regular, 20 pt, with Auto leading and -20 Tracking.

     Click the Character palette icon, as shown

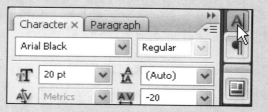

     To collapse the Character palette.

8   With the Horizontal Type tool, drag a marquee approximately as shown, starting at the left title-safe zone guide

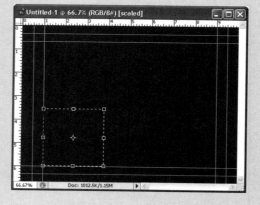

9   Type **Play**

     Press (↵ ENTER) twice

     (Use the Enter key on the alphabetic keypad.) To insert paragraph breaks.

10 Type **Select Scene**

    Press (↵ ENTER) twice

    Type **Special**

    Press (↵ ENTER)

    Type **Features**

    Press (↵ ENTER) on the numeric
    keypad

To insert paragraph breaks.

You'll complete this menu choice on the next line.

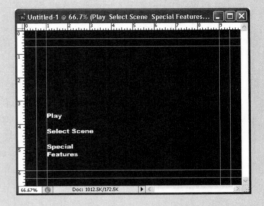

To complete text editing. To verify that Photoshop scaled the type, temporarily turn off pixel aspect ratio correction.

11 Choose **Image**,
    Pixel Aspect Ratio, **Square**

To display the image without simulating a video monitor. The text characters appear wider than normal.

12 Choose **Image**,
    Pixel Aspect Ratio,
    D1/DV NTSC (0.9)

To return the image so it looks as it would on TV.

13 Save the image

In the current unit folder.

Scaling images for video

Explanation

You've seen that square-pixel images won't be displayed correctly in a video production, and you know how to generate a new image with pixel aspect ratio correction. There's still the matter of correcting the problem for existing images, though.

To correct the problem, you need to scale the square-pixel image horizontally in the opposite direction of the video standard's pixel width. For example, for NTSC video, you need to scale the image to 112.5% of its original width (720 pixels / 640 pixels × 100%).

However, there's an easier approach than calculating the amount and scaling it yourself. Dragging a layer from a square-pixel image to one with a non-square pixel aspect ratio will automatically scale the layer horizontally to compensate for the difference in pixel widths.

Before scaling any image for video, you should check to ensure that your video application will not also attempt to adjust for pixel aspect ratio (you don't want to overcompensate). For example, Adobe After Effects will automatically scale square-pixel images other than those created at standard sizes (such as the NTSC DV size of 720 × 480 pixels), so if you create an image at any dimension other than standard sizes, you should *not* scale it in Photoshop. Other video applications might not work the same way, so you might need to change your approach in Photoshop accordingly.

Do it!

A-3: Scaling a square-pixel image for video

Here's how	Here's why
1 Activate the DVD title image window	You need to scale this image for video and incorporate it with the DVD menu image.
Arrange the open image windows	To see both images at the same time.
2 Select the Cooking with layer	If necessary.
Press (SHIFT) and click the Dish layer	To select the three layers you want to add to the menu.
3 Drag one of the selected layers to the center of the DVD menu window	To duplicate the layers in the other image, and to scale them horizontally in the process.
With the Move tool, drag in the image so the Dish layer snaps to the top and right edges of the image	

4 Observe the shape of the dish	The dish still appears circular, despite the difference in pixel aspect ratio.
View the image with a square pixel aspect ratio, and then return to the NTSC ratio	The dish appears wide when the image is displayed with square pixels; this confirms that Photoshop scaled it to compensate for the difference in pixel aspect ratio between the two images.
	The title appears partly outside the title-safe area, so this needs to be corrected.
5 Press (CTRL) and click the Dish layer	To deselect it.
Drag the title to within the title-safe zone	
	The image is now prepared correctly for use in a video application for NTSC output.
6 Update and close all images	

Topic B: Video layers

This topic covers the following Adobe ACE exam objectives for Photoshop CS3.

#	Objective
5.4	Explain how to retouch video by using tools and features in Adobe Photoshop. (Tools and features include: Clone tool, Clone Source panel, and Animation panel.)
7.3	Create and use video layers.

Creating video layers

Explanation

Using Photoshop CS3 Extended, you can open a video file as a video layer. You can edit or paint on individual frames, and you can apply filters, masks, transformations, layer styles, and blending modes to the video layer. You can then save the document as a PSD file, or you can render it as a QuickTime movie.

You can use Photoshop's File, Open command to open a video file. The video file appears as a single layer in the Layers palette, with a video icon on the layer thumbnail, as shown in Exhibit 5-4. In addition, you can create a new video layer in an existing document by choosing either of the following commands:

- Layer, Video Layers, New Video Layer from File
- Layer, Video Layers, New Blank Video Layer

In Photoshop, you can open files in the following QuickTime video formats:

- MPEG-1
- MPEG-4
- MOV
- AVI
- FLV from QuickTime (supported if you have Adobe Flash 8 installed)
- MPEG-2 (supported if an MPEG-2 encoder is installed on your computer)

You must have QuickTime 7.0 or later installed on your computer to work with video in Photoshop CS3 Extended.

Exhibit 5-4: A video layer

The Animation timeline

You can use the Animation palette to view each frame of a video. The Animation palette displays a timeline with playback controls, shown in Exhibit 5-5. To navigate among frames, you can drag the Current Time Indicator, or click the playback controls to move to the first frame, previous frame, or next frame.

After you navigate to a frame, you can use Photoshop's tools to edit and paint on that frame. Photoshop does not apply those changes directly to the original video file stored on your computer. Instead, your edits are made to an instance of the original video.

In addition, you can create a blank video layer above a video layer, and you can then paint in that blank layer rather than painting directly in the original video layer containing the video. That way, you can easily alter or remove your painting edits later. If you want to remove edits that you applied directly to a given video layer frame or to all frames, choose Layer, Video Layers, Restore Frame or choose Layer, Video Layers, Restore All Frames.

You can adjust the entire video by applying an adjustment layer, just as you would apply an adjustment layer for standard Photoshop layers.

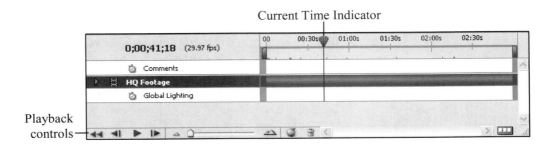

Exhibit 5-5: The Animation palette

Clone options

You can use the Clone Stamp tool to clone parts of a video in one frame, and copy the sampled area to other parts of the same frame, or to other frames. In addition, you can use the Clone Source palette to sample up to five clone sources so you can choose from among them as you paint with the Clone Stamp tool in other areas.

To clone portions of a video:

1   Select the Clone Stamp tool.

2   View the frame from which you want to sample content.

3   Press and hold Alt and click the area you want to sample.

4   Navigate to a frame where you want to paint the sampled area, if necessary.

5   Drag to paint the sampled content in the new location.

To use the Clone Source palette to specify multiple clone sources:

1   Select a Clone Source icon in the Clone Source palette, shown in Exhibit 5-6.

2   Use the Clone Stamp tool to sample part of a frame.

3   Select the next Clone Source icon in the Clone Source palette and sample part of a frame.

4   Repeat step 3 until you've specified up to five clone sources you want to use.

5   To paint from any of the clone sources you've specified, click the appropriate Clone Source icon in the Clone Source palette, and paint with the Clone Stamp tool.

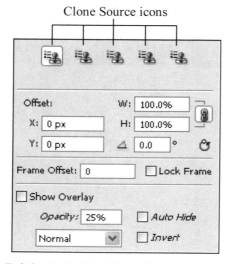

Exhibit 5-6: The Clone Source palette

Exporting a QuickTime file

After working with video layers in Photoshop, you can export the file as a QuickTime movie by choosing File, Export, Render Video. In the Render Video dialog box, you can specify a QuickTime format, and click Render.

Do it!   **B-1:   Discussing video layers**

Questions and answers

1   How can you open a QuickTime video file in Photoshop?

2   To work with video in Photoshop CS3 Extended, what additional software should be installed on your computer?

3   How can you navigate to specific frames in a video file in Photoshop?

4   When you're using the Clone Stamp tool, how can you specify multiple clone sources from which to choose as you paint on frames?

5   After editing video content in Photoshop CS3 Extended, how can you export the content as a new QuickTime movie file?

Unit summary: Video

Topic A   In this topic, you created a new image and adjusted an existing one to use the correct **pixel aspect ratio** for NTSC video so the images appear without distortion.

Topic B   In this topic, you learned how to work with **QuickTime video** content in Photoshop's **video layers**. You also learned how to navigate **video frames** and how to edit the content in video frames.

Independent practice activity

In this activity, you'll create an image for use in a video project. You'll add text to the image, and you'll temporarily disable pixel aspect ratio correction.

1 Create an image named **Video menu practice**. Specify NTSC DV as the size. Specify a black background.

2 Within the title-safe zone, use the Horizontal Type tool to define a marquee as shown in Exhibit 5-7.

3 Specify Arial Black text, 24 pt, with Auto leading.

4 Add the text shown in Exhibit 5-8.

5 View the image as it would appear without pixel aspect ratio correction. (*Hint*: Use the Image, Pixel Aspect Ratio submenu to specify square pixels.)

6 Set the image to display pixel aspect ratio correction again. (*Hint*: Use the D1/DV NTSC (0.9) setting.)

7 Save and close the image.

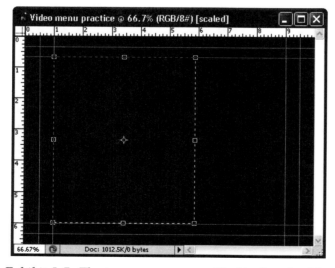

Exhibit 5-7: The type marquee specified in Step 2 of the independent practice activity

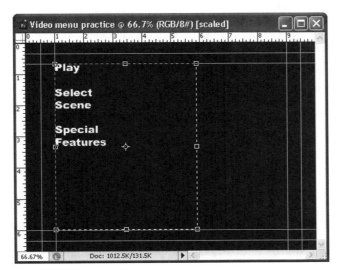

Exhibit 5-8: The type specified in Step 4

Review questions

1 Why might you use Video Preview to display images on a video monitor connected to your computer?

   A To preview differences in how an image appears on a video monitor as compared to on a computer monitor.

   B To preview QuickTime movies embedded in your images.

   C To preview animated GIF images.

   D To preview Flash content.

2 Why might a Photoshop image appear distorted when viewed on a video monitor?

   A Video monitors typically have higher resolution than computer monitors.

   B Video monitors typically display more colors than computer monitors.

   C Computer monitors display images with square pixels, but video monitors use non-square pixels.

   D Computer monitors use square pixels even when displaying images with non-square pixels.

3 Pixel aspect ratio correction is primarily useful for images intended for:

   A Print

   B The Web

   C Video

   D PDF files

4 What is the purpose of displaying an image by using pixel aspect ratio correction?

   A To display the image at its intended print resolution.

   B To display the image at its intended resolution for online display.

   C To display an image as it might appear when distorted by JPEG compression at various quality settings.

   D To display the image using non-square pixels to simulate how it might look on a video monitor.

5 You're preparing an image that will be included in a video that will be viewed on video monitors. What color mode should you use for the image?

   A CMYK

   B 8-bit RGB

   C 16-bit RGB

   D Multichannel

6 You have a QuickTime video file that you want to open in an existing Photoshop file. What should you do?

   A Choose Layer, Video Layers, New Video Layer from File.

   B Choose Layer, Video Layers, New Blank Video Layer.

   C Choose File, Open.

   D Choose File, Place.

7 You have a QuickTime video file that you want to open directly in Photoshop. What should you do?

   A Choose Layer, Video Layers, New Video Layer from File.

   B Choose Layer, Video Layers, New Blank Video Layer.

   C Choose File, Open.

   D Choose File, Place.

8 You want to edit a specific frame in a video layer. Which palette should you use to navigate to that specific video frame?

   A The Actions palette

   B The Animation palette

   C The Channels palette

   D The Navigator palette

9 Which statement about editing video content is *not* true?

   A You can use the Clone Stamp tool to clone parts of a video in one frame, and copy the sampled area to other parts of the same frame, or to other frames.

   B You can use the Clone Source palette to sample an unlimited number of clone sources in video frames.

   C You can edit or paint on individual frames of a video layer.

   D You can apply filters, masks, transformations, layer styles, and blending modes to a video layer.

Unit 6

Automating tasks

Unit time: 50 minutes

Complete this unit, and you'll know how to:

A Use the Actions palette to record, play, and edit actions.

B Display actions as buttons and organize actions into action sets.

C Run an action on multiple images by batch-processing them.

D Customize keyboard shortcuts and menus.

Topic A: Actions

This topic covers the following Adobe ACE exam objectives for Photoshop CS3.

#	Objective
10.1	Create and use actions.
10.3	List and describe the automation features available in Adobe Photoshop.
10.4	Describe the difference between scripting and actions and when you would use one over the other.

Using actions

Explanation

As you work with Photoshop, you might find that you perform certain sets of commands consistently on many images. For example, you might often open an image, apply the Embed Watermark filter to it, and save it in the JPEG format. You can use the Actions palette to create an *action* that performs all of these commands as a single step. You can then run the action at any time on a single image, or you can use a *batch process* to run the action for an entire folder of images.

Action design

When you create actions, be careful to create action steps that will work with a variety of images. For example, if you want an action to double the width of the image in pixels, you should record the action to use a Width setting of 200% in the Image Size dialog box. This will double the size of any image to which the action is applied, regardless of the original width. If instead you recorded the action on an image that was 300 pixels wide, and you entered a width of 600 pixels in the Image Size dialog box, all images you applied the action to would be sized to 600 pixels wide, which wasn't your original intent.

Two of the commands in the File, Automate submenu can help you make actions that will be applicable to a variety of images:

- The Conditional Mode Change command lets you specify conditions under which to change to a specific mode (such as CMYK) from one or more original source modes. For example, you can use this command to create an action that converts only RGB images, not grayscale ones, to CMYK.

- The Fit Image command sizes an image to fit *within* a specified width and height, rather than fitting *exactly to* those dimensions or to a percentage of the original. This command is good for actions applied to several images to make them relatively uniform in size while retaining their original aspect ratios.

If you need more control over automation, you might consider creating scripts (written in JavaScript on either platform, in VBScript for Windows, or in AppleScript for Macintosh) instead of actions. For example, any aspect of a script can be conditional, much like the Conditional Mode Change command, so some steps will run only when conditions you specify are met. Scripts also allow for variables in file paths instead of exact file locations. Scripts can open, rename, and save files, and a single script can involve multiple applications.

Scripting is more complex than creating actions and is beyond the scope of this course. For details, read the *Adobe Photoshop CS3 Scripting Guide*, available at www.adobe.com.

Creating an action

The Actions palette, shown in Exhibit 6-1, includes some default actions that you can use right away. However, you'll probably need to create your own actions to streamline your specific workflows. To create an action, you can use the Actions palette to record a set of commands and steps as you perform them.

To create an action:

1 Open an image that will serve as a good example of the type of images to which you'll apply the action.

2 Perform any steps that are necessary to prepare the image, but that you don't want to record as part of the action.

3 In the Actions palette, click the Create new action button to open the New Action dialog box.

4 Enter a name for the action, specify a keyboard shortcut for running the action, and choose a color for the action's button (for when you display the Actions palette in Button mode).

5 Click Record.

6 Perform the commands and other steps you want the action to record.

7 In the Actions palette, click the Stop playing/recording button to stop recording action steps.

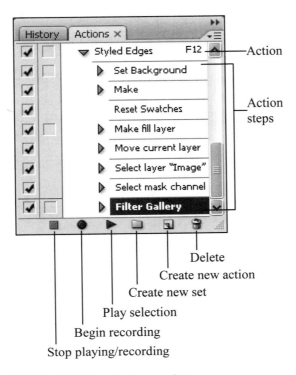

Exhibit 6-1: The Actions palette

Do it!

A-1: Recording an action

Here's how	Here's why
1 Open Lake and mountain	(In the current unit folder.) You'll use this image to record an action that creates a white, stylized frame around an image.
Save the image in Photoshop format as **My lake and mountain**	
2 Verify that the rulers are visible	Before recording the action, you'll create a selection, which the action will use to create a layer mask. Because the layer mask will be a different size and shape for each image to which you apply the action, you won't record the creation of the selection as part of the action.
3 Using the Rectangular Marquee tool, create a selection as shown	
	(Select the Rectangular Marquee tool, and select Normal from the Style list on the options bar.) There should be one inch outside the selection on all sides.
4 Click [▶]	(The Actions palette icon in the collapsed dock of palettes.) To display the Actions palette.
In the Actions palette, click [🗐]	(The Create new action button.) To open the New Action dialog box.
In the Name box, enter **Styled Edges**	
From the Function Key list, select **F12**	
From the Color list, select **Red**	
Click **Record**	The next steps you perform in the image will be recorded as steps in the action you just created.

5 Double-click the Background layer	To open the New Layer dialog box.
In the Name box, enter **Image**	
Click **OK**	You can now manipulate the layer as a regular layer.
6 In the Layers palette, click [□]	(The Add layer mask button.) To add a layer mask using the selection.
Press (D)	To set the foreground and background colors to their defaults.
	You will add a solid-color fill layer that will eventually be used as the background.
7 In the Layers palette, click [⬤].	(The "Create new fill or adjustment layer" button.) To display a menu.
Choose **Solid Color...**	To open the Color Picker.
In the toolbox, click the white Foreground Color swatch	(If necessary.) To select white.
Click **OK**	To create a solid-white fill layer and close the Color Picker.
8 Choose **Layer**, **Arrange**, **Send to Back**	To place the fill layer behind the Image layer.
9 Select the Image layer	
Click the layer mask thumbnail, as shown	

To select it.

10 Choose **Filter**, **Filter Gallery...**	To open the Filter Gallery.
Expand the **Brush Strokes** category	

11 Select **Sprayed Strokes**	To display the Sprayed Strokes settings.
Set the Stroke Length value to **11**	
Set the Spray Radius value to **25**	
Verify that Right Diagonal is selected in the Stroke Direction list	
Click **OK**	To apply the filter.
12 In the Actions palette, click ▣	(The Stop playing/recording button.) To stop recording the action.
13 Drag the bottom edge of the Actions palette down	To enlarge it so you can see all of the steps in the action you just recorded.

Running actions

Explanation

After creating an action, you can run it on other images to perform its steps as a single command, automating your work.

To run an action on a single image:

1 Open the image to which you want to apply the action.
2 Perform any steps necessary to prepare the image for the action.
3 Play the action:

- In the Actions palette, select the action you want to apply, and click the Play selection button.
- Press the keyboard keys you assigned to the action.

Do it!

A-2: Playing an action

Here's how	Here's why
1 Choose **File, Revert**	To restore the image to its original saved state.
2 Using the Rectangular Marquee tool, create a selection marquee similar to the one you created earlier	There should be one inch outside the selection on all sides. Because you created the action after selecting an image area, you need to create a selection again for the action to work properly. However, you could select any image area with any selection tool, and the action would be applied based on that selection.

3 In the Actions palette, select
   Styled Edges

   Click  ▶

(The Play selection button.) To run the action. The action automates the process of creating the stylized edge.

Because the action is not saved as part of a document, but is instead saved with the application, you can apply the action to other images.

   Update the image

4 Open Zesty

In the current unit folder.

   Save the image as **My Zesty**

5 Create an elliptical marquee around the word and vegetables, as shown

6 Play the Styled Edges action

(Select the Styled Edges action in the Actions palette. Then click the Play selection button or press F12, which is the keyboard shortcut you assigned to the action.)

The action steps will run, but the image layers prevent the effect from being displayed properly.

Editing actions

Explanation

After you create an action and run it on several images, you might find that it doesn't work the way you intended for all images. In addition, you might want to adjust some of the action settings to create a slightly different result. You can modify an action by adding, removing, and modifying steps.

To record a new step for an existing action:

1 In the Actions palette, select the step that you want the new step to follow.
2 Click the Begin recording button.
3 Select the command or perform the step you want to add.
4 Click the Stop playing/recording button.

If you want to change the placement of the added step (in the sequence of steps), you can drag it in the Actions palette.

To change dialog-box settings for an action step:

1 In the Actions palette, select the step you want to modify.
2 From the Actions palette menu, choose Record Again to open the dialog box associated with the selected step.
3 Specify the new settings you want the step to use.
4 Click OK.

To remove an action step:

1 Select the step you want to remove.
2 Click the Delete button.
3 Click OK.

Do it!

A-3: Editing an action

Here's how	Here's why
1 Drag the Actions palette's bottom edge down	To make the Actions palette the height of the screen. It's now easier to see and edit the action steps.
2 Select the **Set Background** step, as shown	
	You've seen that this action won't work properly on layered images, so it needs a step to flatten the image. You'll record a new step here to flatten the image before continuing.

3 Click [●]

The Begin recording button.

From the Layers palette menu,
choose **Flatten Image**

Click [■]

To stop recording the action. The newly
recorded Flatten Image step appears after the Set
Background step, but needs to be before it.

Drag the **Flatten Image** step
above the Set Background step

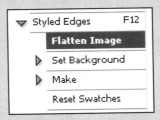

4 Revert the My zesty image

Choose File, Revert.

Create an elliptical selection

Run the Styled Edges action

(Press F12.) This time, the action works
properly.

Next, you'll lower the Spray Radius in the Filter
Gallery and add another filter to make the effect
more interesting.

5 In the History palette, select the
Send To Back step

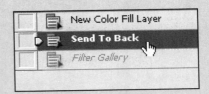

The next-to-last History step.

In the Layers palette, select the
layer mask thumbnail for the
Image layer

In the Actions palette, select the
Filter Gallery step

6 From the Actions palette menu,
choose **Record Again...**

To open the Filter Gallery.

Set the Spray Radius value to **23**

7 Click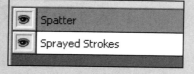

The New effect layer icon, located at the bottom-right edge of the Filter Gallery.

Under Brush Strokes, select **Spatter**

Set the Spray Radius value to **8**

Set the Smoothness value to **4**

8 Verify that the Spatter effect is above the Sprayed Strokes effect in the list

| 👁 | Spatter |
| 👁 | Sprayed Strokes |

Click **OK**

To finish re-recording the Filter Gallery step.

9 In the Actions palette, expand the **Make fill layer** step

Because this step sets the color to Red 255, Green 255, Blue 255, it's unnecessary to have a Reset Swatches step in the beginning of the action. Therefore, you should delete that step so the user doesn't lose the active foreground and background colors.

10 Select the Reset Swatches step

Click 🗑

(The Delete button.) An alert box appears.

Click **OK**

To delete the action step.

11 Revert the image

Create an elliptical marquee in the image

Play the Styled Edges action

Pausing actions

Explanation

Some actions might be hard for someone other than the author to run without an explanation or specific setup instructions. You can insert a message, called a *stop*, to explain the purpose of the action, the type of image for which it was intended, or any necessary steps the user should take before running it. In addition, for steps that use dialog-box values, you can specify that the dialog box opens during the action's playback, so the user can specify settings for that step, customizing the action each time it's used.

To pause an action and insert a stop:

1   In the Actions palette, select the action to which you want to add a stop.

2   From the Actions palette menu, choose Insert Stop to open the Record Stop dialog box.

3   In the Message box, enter the message that you want to display when the action is played.

4   Check Allow Continue if you want users to be able to ignore the message and continue running the action. If you clear Allow Continue, the user will be forced to click Stop, stopping the action's playback. The user can then continue playing the action, however, beginning with the step after the Stop step.

For a step that requires dialog-box settings, you can have the dialog box open during the action's playback. The user can then specify settings for that step, customizing the action each time it's used. To set a step's associated dialog box to open during playback, click the "Toggle dialog on/off" column next to that step, as shown in Exhibit 6-2.

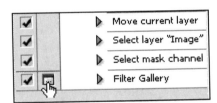

Exhibit 6-2: The "Toggle dialog on/off" column

A-4: Pausing an action

Here's how	Here's why
1 Revert the My Zesty image	
Run the Styled Edges action	Because you didn't select a portion of the image first, an alert box indicates that some of the steps will not run properly.
Click **Stop**	To stop playback of the action. You'll add a step that displays a message telling the user to make a selection before running the action, and warning the user that running the action will flatten the image.
2 Revert the image	
3 In the Actions palette, select the **Styled Edges** action	
4 From the Actions palette menu, choose **Insert Stop...**	To open the Record Stop dialog box.
In the Message box, enter **This action requires a selection prior to running. If you haven't selected an area, please do so now. Also, it flattens the image, so work on a duplicate if you want to retain the original layers.**	
Check **Allow Continue**	To allow users to either stop the action's playback or ignore the message and continue playing the action.
Click **OK**	To create the Stop step.
5 Move **Stop** to the first step in the action, as indicated	
6 Click the "Toggle dialog on/off" column for the Filter Gallery step, as shown	
	To specify that the dialog box associated with this step opens when you play the action, allowing you to change settings each time you run the action.

7 Run the Styled Edges action	The action stops, and a dialog box appears with the message you specified.
Click **Stop**	To stop the action so you can first specify a selection.
8 Create an elliptical marquee in the image	
9 Run the Styled Edges action	The alert message appears. Because you specified a selection, you'll continue the action.
Click **Continue**	When the action gets to the Filter Gallery step, the Filter Gallery dialog box opens. You'll use the current settings.
Click **OK**	To complete the action playback.

Topic B: Organizing actions

This topic covers the following Adobe ACE exam objective for Photoshop CS3.

#	Objective
10.1	Create and use actions.

Methods of organizing actions

Explanation

You might want to organize your actions to make them easier to find and run. You can organize actions into folders called *action sets*, or you can display actions in the Actions palette as a group of buttons.

Button mode

By default, the Actions palette displays actions as a list. You can expand an action to display its steps. You can also set the Actions palette to display the actions as buttons.

When you use Button mode, the actions appear as colored buttons, as shown in Exhibit 6-3. You can then run an action by clicking the button, rather than by selecting an action's name and clicking the Play selection button. In addition, you can find actions more quickly because the individual steps don't appear.

To display the Actions palette in Button mode, choose Button Mode from the Actions palette menu. To return to the default mode, display the Actions palette menu and choose Button Mode again to uncheck it.

Exhibit 6-3: The Actions palette in Button mode

Do it!

B-1:   Making actions work as buttons

Here's how	Here's why
1 From the Actions palette menu, choose **Button Mode**	To display the actions in the palette as buttons.
2 Revert the My Zesty image	
3 Select an area of the image	
4 Click **Styled Edges**	To run the action.
Respond to each dialog box that appears	To finish running the action.

Action sets

Explanation

By default, all actions are stored in an action set named Default Actions. You can create additional action sets to organize your actions into categories.

When you use many actions, organizing them into action sets makes it easier to find a particular action. You can collapse the action sets you don't need at the moment, and expand just the one containing the actions you want, making the Actions palette less cluttered. When you display the Actions palette in Button mode, the buttons from all action sets are displayed together.

Creating action sets

To create an action set, use either of these techniques:

- In the Actions palette, click the Create new set button to create a set named Set 1. You can rename a set by double-clicking its name and entering a new one. (The Create new set button isn't available in Button mode.)
- From the Actions palette menu, choose New Set to open the New Set dialog box. Enter a name and click OK.

To add an action to a set, drag the action to the set's folder icon in the Actions palette.

Sharing actions

After creating actions, you can share them with other Photoshop users. To share the actions in an action set:

1　In the Actions palette, select the action set containing the actions you want to share.

2　From the Actions palette menu, choose Save Actions to open the Save dialog box.

3　Click Save to save the action set as a file.

4　Copy the saved action-set file to the computer where you want to use it.

5　Start Photoshop. From the Actions palette menu, choose Load Actions to open the Load dialog box.

6　Select the action-set file you want to load, and click Load to add it to the Actions palette.

In addition, you can load action sets that come with Photoshop CS3 by loading them from the Adobe Photoshop CS3\Presets\Actions folder.

Do it!

B-2: Saving actions in sets

Here's how	Here's why
1 From the Actions palette menu, choose **Button Mode**	To turn off Button mode. You'll duplicate the Styled Edges action and modify the duplicate to add a white fill layer behind other layers. This is convenient for when you want to create effects such as silhouettes.
2 Click the arrow to the left of the Styled Edges action	To collapse the steps.
Drag the Styled Edges action to the ⬓ icon	(Create new action.) To create a duplicate. The duplicate is named "Styled Edges copy."
Double-click the name **Styled Edges copy**	To select it.
Type **White fill layer background** and press ⏎ ENTER	To rename the duplicate action.
3 Expand the **White fill layer background** action	You'll delete all of the steps except the ones that make a white fill layer and move the layer to the back.
Press CTRL and click each action step, except for Make fill layer and Move current layer	To select the steps.
Click 🗑	A dialog box appears, asking you to verify that you want to delete these steps.
Click **OK**	To remove the selected steps.
4 Collapse the steps for the White fill layer background action	Click the triangle to the left of the name.
5 In the Actions palette, click ▢	(The Create new set button.) To open the New Set dialog box.
In the Name box, enter **My Actions**	
Click **OK**	To create the set.
6 Drag the **Styled Edges** action to the My Actions folder icon	To add the action to the set.
Add the **White fill layer background** action to the set	

Topic C: Batch processing

This topic covers the following Adobe ACE exam objective for Photoshop CS3.

#	Objective
10.2	Create and use batches.

The Batch command

Explanation

In many instances, you might want to run an action on several images. For example, you might create an action to size images uniformly for printing or the Web. It would be tedious to apply such actions to each image individually; instead, you can *batch-process* them to let Photoshop apply the action to all of them in sequence without your intervention.

You can perform a batch process in Photoshop by choosing File, Automate, Batch, or you can perform a batch process in Adobe Bridge by choosing Tools, Photoshop, Batch in Adobe Bridge. In the Batch dialog box, shown in Exhibit 6-4, you can select the following:

- The action to run.
- The source from which to draw images. The source can be a folder of files, an import source (such as a scanner), files already open in Photoshop, or selected files in Adobe Bridge. You can specify whether to include folders in the selected folder and how to handle issues that arise when images are opened.
- The destination in which to save the results. You can save and close the original file or save the results to a folder. You can specify how the batch process should name files and how it should handle errors that occur when the action is run.

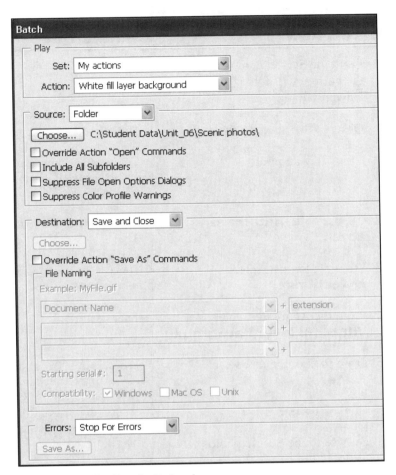

Exhibit 6-4: The Batch dialog box

C-1: Batch-processing files

Here's how	Here's why
1 From the Scenic photos folder in the current unit folder, open Hawaii photo	
Observe the Layers palette	The image has only one layer.
Close Hawaii photo	You'll add a white fill layer to each of the files in the Scenic photos folder to prepare them for masking areas with a white background.
2 Choose **File, Automate, Batch...**	To open the Batch dialog box.
3 From the Set list, select **My actions**	(If necessary.) The action to add the fill layer is in the set you created.
4 From the Action list, select **White fill layer background**	If necessary.
5 From the Source list, select **Folder**	(If necessary.) To run the action on all of the images in a selected folder.
Click **Choose**	To open the Browse for Folder dialog box.
Browse to the Scenic photos folder in the current unit folder	
Click **OK**	To select the Scenic photos folder.
6 From the Destination list, select **Save and Close**	To make the batch process store the results of the action in the original files it opens.
7 Click **OK**	To run the batch process on the Scenic photos folder.
8 Open Hawaii photo	The image now contains a Color fill 1 layer behind the Photo layer that was there before you ran the batch process. At this point, you could run a new action on this and other images, with the fill layer having been created.
9 Close Hawaii photo	

Topic D: Customizing Photoshop

This topic covers the following Adobe ACE exam objective for Photoshop CS3.

#	Objective
1.1	List and describe options available for customizing the user interface. (Options include: using Workspaces, managing panels, docking panels, and customizing menus and shortcuts.)

Customizing keyboard shortcuts and menu colors

Explanation

It's a good idea to memorize the keyboard shortcuts for the commands you use often. In addition, you can create keyboard shortcuts for commands that don't have default shortcuts. You can also customize the appearance of menu commands to make it easier to find the ones you need.

Customizing keyboard shortcuts

To assign a keyboard shortcut:

1 Open the Keyboard Shortcuts and Menus dialog box and activate the Keyboard Shortcuts tab. To do so, use either of these methods:

- Choose Edit, Keyboard Shortcuts.
- Choose Window, Workspace, Keyboard Shortcuts & Menus, and activate the Keyboard Shortcuts tab.

2 Expand the category containing the command you want.

3 Click the command for which you want to add a keyboard shortcut.

4 With the Shortcut box activated, press the keys you want to assign as the shortcut. If the shortcut is already used by another command, assigning it to this command will remove it from the previous command.

5 Click Accept.

After customizing keyboard shortcuts, you can save the current assignments as a keyboard shortcut set. That way, you can create multiple sets that you and other users can switch among.

To switch among keyboard shortcut sets, open the Keyboard Shortcuts and Menus dialog box and select the desired set from the Set list. If you want to return to the default set of keyboard shortcuts, choose Window, Workspace, Reset Keyboard Shortcuts.

Customizing menu command colors

You can use the Keyboard Shortcuts and Menus dialog box to customize the appearance of commands in the menu bar. You can specify that a particular menu item not appear in the menu, or you can apply a color to a menu item. Adding a color to a menu item can make it easier to find the commands you use most often.

To customize the appearance of menu-bar items:

    1 Open the Keyboard Shortcuts and Menus dialog box and activate the Menus tab. To do so, use either of these methods:

- Choose Edit, Menus.
- Choose Window, Workspace, Keyboard Shortcuts & Menus, and activate the Menus tab.

    2 Expand the category containing the command you want to customize.

    3 Click the command whose appearance you want to customize.

    4 Specify options for the item's appearance.

- If you want to hide the item (have it not appear in the menu), click the eye icon in the Visibility column.
- If you want to change the item's color, click in the Color column to open the Color list. Select the color you want to apply to the menu item.

    5 Click OK.

As with keyboard shortcuts, you can save your menu customizations as a set, which you can then switch among, depending on your needs. To return to the default set, choose Window, Workspace, Reset Menus.

Do it!

D-1: Assigning keyboard shortcuts and menu item colors

Here's how	Here's why
1 Choose **Edit, Keyboard Shortcuts...**	To open the Keyboard Shortcuts and Menus dialog box with the Keyboard Shortcuts tab activated.
2 Expand the Window category	You'll assign a keyboard shortcut to the History command in the Window menu so you can quickly show and hide the History palette.
Scroll in the commands list until you see History	
Select **History**	The Shortcut box for the History command is active.
Press (F9)	An alert appears, telling you that F9 is already in use and that assigning it to this command will remove it from the Window, Actions command.
Press (ALT) + (SHIFT) + (F9)	This keyboard shortcut is not being used by any other command.
Click **Accept**	You will save the modified keyboard shortcuts in a new set.

3 Click  🖫	(The "Create a new set based on the current set of shortcuts" button.) To open the Save dialog box.
In the File Name box, enter **Action editing shortcuts**	
Click **Save**	To save the set.
4 Activate the Menus tab	You will apply a color to several menu items to make them easier to see.
Expand the Window category	
Select **Actions**	
In the Color column next to Actions, click **None**	To view the Color list.
From the Color list, select **Red**	
Apply the Red color to the **History** menu item	
5 Click  🖫	To open the Save dialog box.
In the File Name box, enter **Action editing menus**	
Click **Save**	
Click **OK**	
6 Click the Window menu	Observe that the Actions and History commands are red, and the new keyboard shortcut appears next to the History command.

Workspaces

Explanation

After you customize menus, specify keyboard shortcuts, and customize the position and grouping of palettes, you can save the current configuration as a new workspace. That way, you can create several workspaces for different users or workflows, and you can easily switch among them.

When you choose Window, Workspace, Save Workspace to open the Save Workspace dialog box, you can check Palette Locations, Keyboard Shortcuts, and Menus to specify which of these settings you want to save as part of the workspace. Enter a name for the workspace in the Name box, and then click Save.

Do it!

D-2: Saving a workspace

Here's how	Here's why
1 Choose **Window, Workspace, Save Workspace...**	To open the Save Workspace dialog box.
In the Name box, enter **Action editing**	
Check all three check boxes	
	To save palette locations, keyboard shortcuts, and menus as part of the workspace.
Click **Save**	To save the workspace.
2 Choose **Window, Workspace, Default Workspace**	To return to Photoshop's default palette settings, keyboard shortcuts, and menu items.
Observe the Window menu	To see that the menu items use the default appearance.
3 Choose **Window, Workspace, Action editing**	A dialog box appears, indicating that the selected workspace will modify menu and/or keyboard shortcut sets.
Click **Yes**	To apply the workspace.
4 Observe the Window menu	To see that the custom keyboard shortcut and menu settings are restored.
5 Update and close all images	

Unit summary: Automating tasks

Topic A   In this topic, you recorded an **action** to automate a multiple-step procedure. You also ran an action and modified action steps. Finally, you added **stops** to an action and specified that certain dialog boxes appear during an action's playback.

Topic B   In this topic, you displayed actions as **buttons** and clicked an action button to play it. You also organized actions into **action sets**.

Topic C   In this topic, you used a **batch process** to run an action on multiple files.

Topic D   In this topic, you created **keyboard shortcuts** for commands and specified colors for menu items. You also saved custom keyboard shortcuts, customized menus, and palette configurations as a **workspace**.

Independent practice activity

In this activity, you'll create an action, edit the action steps, and run the action.

1 Create an image with pixel dimensions of 400×400, a transparent background, and the Set Pixel Aspect Ratio set to Square Pixels.

2 Add a layer to the image (so you can eventually record an action step to bring a layer to the front after you create a layer that's not in front). Select the bottom layer.

3 Create an action named **Star field** with the following steps:

    a   Create a layer, and then choose **Layer**, **Arrange**, **Bring to Front**.

    b   Choose **Select**, **All**; press Shift+Backspace to open the Fill dialog box; select Black for the fill color; and click **OK**.

    c   Choose **Filter**, **Noise**, **Add Noise**; specify an amount of **16**; select **Gaussian** distribution; check **Monochromatic**; and click **OK**.

    d   Choose **Edit**, **Transform**, **Scale**. On the options bar, click the link icon between the W and H boxes to make them both change when you enter a value. Enter **200** in the W box, and press Enter twice.

    e   Choose **Image**, **Adjustments**, **Levels** and specify Input levels of **40**, **0.70**, and **140**.

4 Stop recording.

5 Before the Levels step, add a stop with the text **Drag the midtone slider to change star density**. Allow users to continue.

6 Toggle the dialog on for the Levels step.

7 Duplicate the Levels step. (*Hint*: Drag it to the Create new action button).

8 Create an image with pixel dimensions of 800×800, and run the Star field action. When the message box appears, click **Continue**. In the Levels dialog box, drag the midtone slider to specify the midtone you want, and click **OK**. In the second Levels dialog box that appears, drag the midtone slider, and click **OK** to finish running the action.

9 Close all images without saving them.

10 Close Photoshop.

Review questions

1 If you need to make any step in an automated process conditional, you should create a(n):

   A Script

   B Action

   C Batch process

   D Preset

2 When might you choose to automate a task by using a script instead of an action? [Choose all that apply.]

   A When the task includes many steps that you want to set up with conditions.

   B When you want to automate a simple task without using JavaScript code, VBScript, or AppleScript.

   C When the task involves several applications in addition to Photoshop.

   D When you want to record a series of steps you perform in Photoshop.

3 How can you create a Photoshop action?

   A Write out the action by using JavaScript code.

   B Use the Actions palette to record a series of steps as you perform them in Photoshop.

   C Write out the action by using VBScript for Windows or AppleScript for Macintosh.

   D Choose Edit, Menus, and specify the commands you want to use in the action.

4 Which of these statements about Photoshop actions are true? [Choose all that apply.]

   A To make an action pause to display a message or warning, you can insert a stop.

   B When you display the Actions palette in Button mode, you can run an action with a single click.

   C You can save an individual action without having to save a set.

   D An action can include steps involving several applications in addition to Photoshop.

5 Which of these are possible sources for images you want to batch-process? [Choose all that apply.]

   A A folder of files, including the contents of subfolders

   B Selected files in Adobe Bridge

   C Multiple folders stored in different locations on your computer

   D Files already open in Photoshop

6 How can you run an action on multiple files at once?

    A Run the action from the Actions palette.

    B Run the action in Button mode.

    C Choose File, Automate, Batch.

    D Drag the files to the Actions palette.

7 True or false: A batch process must store the results of the action in another location, not in the original files.

8 Which are benefits of creating multiple workspaces? [Choose all that apply.]

    A You can lock all palettes so they can't be moved.

    B You can customize the organization of palettes for various workflows.

    C You can specify a password to restrict access to your workspace.

    D When several people share a computer, you can customize the palette locations for each person.

9 Which of these can you perform by changing the workspace? [Choose all that apply.]

    A Apply colors to palettes.

    B Change palette positions.

    C Make some menu items invisible.

    D Change keyboard shortcuts.

10 True or false: You can change the colors of menu items.

11 How can you customize keyboard shortcuts?

    A Choose Edit, Preferences.

    B Choose Edit, Menus.

    C Choose Edit, Keyboard Shortcuts.

    D Right-click a command, enter the keyboard shortcut you want it to use, and click OK.

12 How can you customize menus by using the Menus tab in the Keyboard Shortcuts and Menus dialog box? [Choose all that apply.]

    A You can move menu commands from one menu to another.

    B You can specify that a menu command be displayed in a particular color.

    C You can specify that a menu command no longer appear in the menu.

    D You can choose a new font for all menu commands.

Appendix A

ACE exam objectives map

This appendix provides the following information:

A ACE exam objectives for Photoshop CS3 with references to corresponding coverage in ILT Series courseware.

Topic A: Comprehensive exam objectives

Explanation
The following table lists the Adobe Certified Expert (ACE) exam objectives for Photoshop CS3 and indicates where each objective is covered in conceptual explanations, hands-on activities, or both.

#	Objective	Course level	Conceptual information	Supporting activities
1.1	List and describe options available for customizing the user interface. (Options include: using Workspaces, managing panels, docking panels, customizing menus and shortcuts)	Basic	Unit 1, Topic B	B-2
		Advanced	Unit 6, Topic D	D-1, D-2
1.2	Given a scenario, create a tool preset.	Advanced	Unit 1, Topic B	B-4, B-5
1.3	Given a scenario, select the appropriate color mode for an image. (Scenarios include for Web, Video, Print, and Mobile)	Basic	Unit 4, Topic A	A-1, A-2
		Advanced	Unit 5, Topic A	
		Print	Unit 4, Topic A	A-1
			Unit 5, Topic A	A-2
			Unit 5, Topic C	C-1
		Web Design	Unit 1, Topic B	
1.4	Add metadata for an image in Adobe Photoshop.	Basic	Unit 7, Topic B	B-2
1.5	Explain the advantages of and when you would use 32-bit, 16-bit, and 8-bit images.	Basic	Unit 4, Topic A	A-1
		Color Printing	Unit 2, Topic A	
			Unit 2, Topic D	
1.6	Explain how to use filters and the Filter Gallery.	Basic	Unit 5, Topic D	D-1
		Web Design	Unit 1, Topic A	A-2
2.1	Given a tool, paint on a layer by using that tool. (tools include: Brush Tool, Pencil Tool, Eraser)	Basic	Unit 5, Topic B	B-3
			Unit 5, Topic C	C-1, C-2
2.2	Given a tool, retouch an image by using that tool. (tools include: Spot Healing Brush, Healing Brush, Patch Tool, Clone Source panel)	Basic	Unit 5, Topic A	A-1, A-2, A-3, A-4, A-5
2.3	Adjust the tonal range of an image by using an adjustment layer. (Options include: Levels, Curves, Brightness/Contrast, Black & White)	Basic	Unit 4, Topic C	C-1, C-2, C-3
		Color Printing	Unit 3, Topic B	B-2
			Unit 3, Topic C	C-3
			Unit 3, Topic D	D-1, D-2, D-3
			Unit 4, Topic C	C-1
			Unit 5, Topic A	A-1

#	Objective	Course level	Conceptual information	Supporting activities
2.4	Explain how blending modes are used to control how pixels are effected when using a painting or editing tool.	Basic	Unit 5, Topic B	B-3
2.5	Create and use gradients and patterns.	Advanced	Unit 1, Topic B Unit 1, Topic C	B-1, B-2, B-3 C-1
2.6	Create and edit a custom brush.	Advanced	Unit 4, Topic A	A-3
3.1	Create and arrange layers and groups.	Basic	Unit 3, Topic A Unit 3, Topic B Unit 3, Topic C	A-1, A-2, A-3 B-1 C-1, C-2
		Advanced	Unit 4, Topic C	C-1
3.2	Explain the purpose of layer comps and when you would use a layer comp.	Advanced	Unit 4, Topic E	E-1
3.3	Explain how or why you would use a clipping group.	Basic	Unit 4, Topic C	C-3
		Advanced	Unit 2, Topic D	D-1
3.4	Explain how or why you would use a layer mask.	Advanced	Unit 2, Topic B Unit 2, Topic C	B-1, B-2 C-1, C-2
3.5	Create and save a layer style.	Basic	Unit 3, Topic D	D-3
3.6	Given a scenario, select, align, and distribute multiple layers in an image.	Basic	Unit 3, Topic A Unit 3, Topic B	A-3 B-1
4.1	Create and modify selections by using the appropriate selection tool. (Selection tools include: Quick Selection, Lasso, Magic Wand, Marquee)	Basic	Unit 2, Topic A Unit 2, Topic B	A-1, A-2, A-4, A-5, A-6, A-7 A-8 B-1, B-2, B-3
4.2	Save and load selections.	Basic	Unit 2, Topic A	A-3
4.3	Modify and preview a selection by using Refine Edge.	Basic	Unit 2, Topic B	B-4
4.4	Create and modify selections by using the Channels palette.	Basic	Unit 2, Topic A	
		Advanced	Unit 2, Topic A	A-2
5.1	Given a scenario create a new document by selecting the appropriate document preset.	Advanced	Unit 1, Topic A Unit 5, Topic A	A-2 A-2
5.2	Explain the purpose of Video Preview.	Advanced	Unit 5, Topic A	
5.3	Describe the purpose of pixel aspect ratio correction.	Advanced	Unit 5, Topic A	A-1, A-2, A-3
5.4	Explain how to retouch video by using tools and features in Adobe Photoshop. (Tools and features include: Clone tool, Clone Source panel, Animation panel)	Advanced	Unit 5, Topic B	

#	Objective	Course level	Conceptual information	Supporting activities
6.1	Create shape layers and paths by using the Pen and Shape tools.	Advanced	Unit 3, Topic A Unit 3, Topic B Unit 3, Topic D	A-4 B-2, B-3 D-3
6.2	Explain the advantages of using vector drawing tools versus using raster drawing tools.	Advanced	Unit 3, Topic A	A-1
6.3	Given a scenario, alter the properties of type.	Basic Advanced	Unit 3, Topic C Unit 3, Topic D	C-3 D-1 D-2
6.4	Create and edit paths by using the Paths palette.	Advanced	Unit 3, Topic A Unit 3, Topic C	A-2, A-3 C-2
7.1	Create and use Smart Objects. (Smart Objects include: vector, raster, and camera Raw files)	Advanced	Unit 4, Topic C	C-2, C-3, C-4
7.2	Convert content to be used with Smart Filters. (Options include: applying filters, masking filters, editing and deleting filters)	Advanced Color Printing	Unit 4, Topic D Unit 2, Topic A	D-1, D-2 A-1
7.3	Create and use video layers.	Advanced	Unit 5, Topic B	
7.4	Import, transform, and edit textures on 3D layers.	Advanced	Unit 4, Topic F	F-1
8.1	List and describe the functionality Adobe Bridge provides for viewing assets.	Basic	Unit 1, Topic B	B-4
8.2	Explain how to apply metadata and keywords to assets in Adobe Bridge.	Basic	Unit 7, Topic B	B-3
8.3	Given a scenario, select and use the appropriate automation function from the Tools menu in Adobe Bridge. (Scenarios include: stitching panoramic photos, batch renaming images, automating image conversions)	Color Printing	Unit 2, Topic D	D-1
8.4	List and describe the functionality and set the appropriate options in the Camera Raw Preferences dialog box and the Develop Settings menu.	Color Printing	Unit 2, Topic A	A-2
9.1	List and describe the advantages of the Camera Raw format and the Digital Negative Converter.	Color Printing	Unit 2, Topic A	A-1
9.2	Given a Camera Raw adjustment setting, explain the purpose of that setting.	Color Printing	Unit 2, Topic A	A-1
9.3	Explain the purpose of and functionality provided by the Open, Save, and Done buttons in the Camera Raw dialog box.	Color Printing	Unit 2, Topic A	A-1

#	Objective	Course level	Conceptual information	Supporting activities
9.4	Explain the functionality provided by High Dynamic Range (HDR) images and describe the workflow for HDR files.	Color Printing	Unit 2, Topic D	D-2, D-3
10.1	Create and use actions.	Advanced	Unit 6, Topic A	A-1, A-2, A-3 A-4
			Unit 6, Topic B	B-1
		Web Design	Unit 4, Topic B	B-1
10.2	Create and use batches.	Advanced	Unit 6, Topic C	C-1
10.3	List and describe the automation features available in Adobe Photoshop.	Basic	Unit 7, Topic C	C-2, C-3
		Advanced	Unit 6, Topic A	
		Print	Unit 2, Topic D	D-1
		Web Design	Unit 4, Topic B	B-2
			Unit 4, Topic C	C-1, C-2
10.4	Describe the difference between scripting and actions and when you would use one over the other.	Advanced	Unit 6, Topic A	
11.1	Discuss the color management workflow process that is used in Adobe Photoshop. (topics include: ICC profiles, color management engine, color numbers)	Color Printing	Unit 1, Topic A	A-2
			Unit 1, Topic B	B-1
			Unit 1, Topic C	C-1
			Unit 1, Topic D	D-1, D-2
11.2	Describe the difference between assigning and converting to ICC profiles.	Color Printing	Unit 1, Topic A	A-2
			Unit 1, Topic C	C-1
11.3	Configure color settings by using the Color Settings dialog box.	Color Printing	Unit 1, Topic C	C-1
			Unit 4, Topic A	A-2, A-3, A-4
11.4	Explain the purpose of and how to use the Proof Setup command.	Color Printing	Unit 1, Topic D	D-1
11.5	Discuss the relationship between color gamut and rendering intents.	Color Printing	Unit 1, Topic D	D-2
12.1	Given a method in the Print dialog box, explain when you would use that method.	Color Printing	Unit 1, Topic D	D-2
12.2	Given a scenario, select and explain when to use a specific Print command (Print commands include: Print One Copy, Print)	Basic	Unit 7, Topic C	C-1
12.3	Explain the differences between monitor, and device resolution.	Basic	Unit 6, Topic A	
13.1	Given a scenario, choose the appropriate file format to optimize images for the Web.	Basic	Unit 7, Topic A	A-1
		Web Design	Unit 1, Topic B	B-1, B-2
			Unit 1, Topic C	C-1, C-2
			Unit 1, Topic D	D-1, D-2, D-3

#	Objective	Course level	Conceptual information	Supporting activities
13.2	Create transparent and matted images by using the Save for Web command.	Web Design	Unit 1, Topic D	D-1, D-2, D-3
13.3	Explain the purpose of and how to use Variables.	Web Design	Unit 4, Topic D	D-1, D-2, D-3
13.4	Explain how slices can be used to optimize images for the Web. (options include: layer based, user slices, linking slices for optimization)	Web Design	Unit 2, Topic A Unit 2, Topic B Unit 2, Topic C Unit 2, Topic D	B-1, B-2, B-3, B-4 C-1 D-1, D-2
13.5	Explain the use of layers when creating an animation in Photoshop.	Web Design	Unit 5, Topic A	A-1, A-3
13.6	Explain how to preview content for a mobile device by using Device Central.	Web Design	Unit 3, Topic B	B-1, B-2

Course summary

This summary contains information to help you bring the course to a successful conclusion. Using this information, you will be able to:

A Use the summary text to reinforce what you've learned in class.

B Determine the next courses in this series (if any), as well as any other resources that might help you continue to learn about Photoshop CS3.

Topic A: Course summary

Use the following summary text to reinforce what you've learned in class.

Unit summaries

Unit 1

In this unit, you added **swatches** to the Swatches palette and applied colors to selections. You also used **fill layers** to create layers filled with solid color. In addition, you learned how to add gradient fills to selections and layers. You also created simple **patterns** and offset patterns. You created custom presets and saved sets of presets with the **Preset Manager**. Finally, you learned how to use **overlay layer styles** to fill layer content with a color, gradient, or pattern.

Unit 2

In this unit, you painted in **Quick Mask mode** and in **alpha channels** to create and modify selections. You also created and modified **layer masks** to hide part of a layer. In addition, you created **grayscale masks** to partially mask part of an image. Finally, you applied a **clipping mask** to mask one layer based on the contents of the layer below.

Unit 3

In this unit, you created and modified **vector paths** and saved paths in the Paths palette. You also reshaped vector paths by manipulating anchor points, direction points, and segments and by adding and removing anchor points. In addition, you used **vector masks** to mask layer content, and you designated a path as a **clipping path**. Finally, you **converted type characters to shapes**, added type along a path, created **vector-based shapes**, applied layer styles to shapes, and created brush strokes that flowed along paths.

Unit 4

In this unit, you used the Art History Brush tool to **simulate a painted effect**, and you applied a Texturizer filter to an Overlay blending-mode layer to **simulate a textured surface**. You also **warped** a text layer and applied preset and custom warps to image content. In addition, you **grouped layers** and converted layers to **Smart Objects**. You also applied filters as **Smart Filters**, and created and exported **layer comps**. Finally, you learned how to import, transform, and edit textures on **3D layers**.

Unit 5

In this unit, you learned how to prepare images for use in **video** productions. In addition, you learned how to open QuickTime video content in **video layers**, and edit video-frame content.

Unit 6

In this unit, you recorded an **action** to automate a multiple-step procedure. You also ran and modified actions, displayed actions as buttons, organized actions into action sets, and **batch-processed** images with actions. In addition, you created **keyboard shortcuts** and specified colors for menu items. Finally, you saved custom keyboard shortcuts, customized menus, and palette configurations as a **custom workspace**.

Topic B: Continued learning after class

It is impossible to learn to use any software effectively in a single day. To get the most out of this class, you should begin working with Photoshop CS3 to perform real tasks as soon as possible. We also offer resources for continued learning.

Next courses in this series

This is the second course in this series. The next courses in this series are:

- *Photoshop CS3: Color Printing, ACE Edition*
    - Manage color for print images
    - Maximize digital image quality
    - Merge images to form panoramas or High Dynamic Range images
    - Apply color correction techniques
    - Separate images into CMYK components
    - Convert images among color modes
- *Photoshop CS3: Web Design, ACE Edition*
    - Optimize images for Web use
    - Slice images
    - Apply links
    - Automate Web tasks
    - Create animation

Other resources

For more information, visit www.axzopress.com.

Photoshop CS3: Advanced

Quick reference

Button	Shortcut keys	Function
	← BACKSPACE	Fills a selection on the Background layer with the background color. On other layers, pressing Backspace removes pixels, creating empty areas.
	ALT + ← BACKSPACE	Fills a selection with the foreground color.
	CTRL + ← BACKSPACE	Fills a selection on any layer with the background color.
	SHIFT + ← BACKSPACE	Opens the Fill dialog box.
	CTRL + A	Selects an entire image.
	D	Sets the foreground and background colors to their defaults.
	X	Switches the foreground and background colors.
	CTRL + SHIFT + J	Creates a Layer via Cut.
	CTRL + J	Creates a Layer via Copy.
	CTRL + D	Deselects the selection.
	CTRL + T	Displays transform handles on the current layer or selection.
	G	Gradient tool — Applies a gradient.
	T	Horizontal Type tool — Creates a type layer, on which you can add text.
	Q	Edit in Quick Mask Mode — Enables Quick Mask mode, in which you specify selections by painting.
	Q	Edit in Standard Mode — Enables Standard editing mode, in which a selection appears as a marquee.
	B	Brush tool — Paints with the foreground color, using a standard or custom brush.

Button	Shortcut keys	Function
	Y	History Brush tool — Paints a copy of pixels selected from a specified history state.
	Y	Art History Brush tool — Paints a copy of pixels from a specified history state, but with stylized paint effects added.
	V	Move tool — Drags the contents of a layer or selection to a new location in the image or to another image.
	A	Path Selection tool — Selects and drags an entire path to move it.
	A	Direct Selection tool — Selects a segment of a path.
	P	Freeform Pen tool — Creates a freeform vector path.
	P	Pen tool — Specifies the positioning of the anchor and direction points that define a vector path.
	M	Rectangular Marquee tool — Makes a rectangular selection.
	M	Elliptical Marquee tool — Makes an elliptical selection.
	L	Lasso tool — Makes freehand selections.
	W	Magic Wand tool — Selects regions of pixels of similar brightness.
	C	Crop tool — Crops an image to change the canvas size.

Glossary

Action

A saved series of steps that Photoshop can perform in sequence with a single click in the Actions palette.

Action set

A group of actions stored as a file, which you can distribute to other users.

Alpha channel

An additional channel that does not contribute to the image itself, as do color channels.

Anchor point

Points along a vector path through which the path flows, much like the dots in a connect-the-dots drawing.

Batch process

The process of running an action on multiple images, storing the results either with the original image files or as new files in a specified folder.

Clipping mask

A combination of layers in which the top layer's contents are visible only over the pixels in the underlying layer.

Clipping path

A vector path that determines which parts of an image should be transparent when the image is placed in a document in another application.

Comp

A version of a document, typically created to show to a client. See *Layer comp*.

Compositing

Combining multiple images, often for the purpose of creating a new realistic image.

Corner point

An anchor point on a vector path in which two segments flow in different directions. The direction points for a corner point don't have to face exactly opposite one another.

Direction point

A point that extends from an anchor point on a vector path and determines the curvature of the adjoining segment.

Fill layer

A special type of layer that can contain a solid color, a gradient, or a pattern, and that automatically expands to fill the image if you change its canvas size.

Flatness value

A value that designates how many small straight segments a PostScript printer should use in simulating a smooth curve. The higher the value, the fewer the segments.

Gradient

A blend of two or more colors in which the colors fade gradually from one to another.

Group

A container in the Layers palette that can store multiple layers so you can manipulate them together and collapse them to one item in the palette.

HSB color model

A three-channel color model that defines colors based on their hue, saturation, and brightness.

Layer comp

A stored version of the Layers palette in a specified state. You can change multiple layers' visibility, position, and appearance with one click by displaying a different layer comp.

Layer mask

A grayscale component that's added to a layer to designate each pixel's visibility. A black pixel in a layer mask makes the corresponding image pixel invisible; a white layer-mask pixel makes the image pixel fully visible.

Masking

Selecting pixels for the purpose of partially or fully obscuring them from view.

NTSC

The television broadcasting standard created by the National Television Standards Committee and used in the United States, Japan, Korea, and Mexico.

Overlay

A fill, gradient, or pattern applied to a layer through a layer style.

Pattern

A saved rectangular design of pixels that you can use for filling or painting as adjacent tiles in an image.

Pixel aspect ratio

The width of a pixel relative to its height. Computer monitors have a square pixel aspect ratio; NTSC video monitors have a 0.9 pixel aspect ratio, with narrow pixels.

Preset

A stored swatch, gradient, pattern, brush, style, contour, custom shape, or tool setting. Photoshop comes with presets, and you can create your own.

Quick Mask mode

A mode that displays a selection as a semi-transparent overlay to differentiate between selected and non-selected image areas.

Safe zones

Areas within a video frame in which you can safely display text or action without concern for them being cut off because of television overscan.

Segment

The part of a vector path between two anchor points.

Shape layer

A layer consisting of a fill and a vector mask, which creates the appearance of a filled shape within the mask edges.

Smart Filter

A filter applied to a Smart Object layer so that the filter is applied nondestructively.

Smart Object

An object that acts as a layer but stores the original image data of one or more layers. Smart Objects allow you to transform an image to smaller sizes and then back to the original size with no loss in quality.

Smooth point

An anchor point on a vector path in which the segments on either side curve in the same direction. Smooth points have direction points that face exactly opposite one another.

Snapshot

A saved history state that appears at the top of the History palette.

State

A step that appears in the History palette and represents the version of the image after that step was performed.

Stop

An action step that pauses the action and displays a message to the user.

Subpath

A secondary path created along with an existing path in the Paths palette. Subpaths can add to, subtract from, intersect with, or exclude original path areas, depending on the option selected.

Swatch

A color saved in the Swatches palette.

Vector mask

A vector path component added to a layer to designate each pixel's visibility, much like a layer mask does.

Vector path

A geometric shape, such as a smoothly flowing curve, defined by a series of points with segments between them.

Warp

A transformation you can apply to text or image layers that reshapes the content. You can create warps based on preset shapes or by dragging handles.

Index